SOLVING
TEACHING PROBLEMS

Goodyear Education Series

Theodore W. Hipple, Editor
UNIVERSITY OF FLORIDA

Change for Children: Ideas and Activities
for Individual Learning
SANDRA NINA KAPLAN, JO ANN BUTOM KAPLAN,
SHEILA KUNISHIMA MADSEN and BETTE K. TAYLOR

Crucial Issues in Contemporary Education
THEODORE W. HIPPLE

Elementary School Teaching: Problems and Methods
MARGARET KELLY GIBLIN

Popular Media and the Teaching of English
THOMAS R. GIBLIN

School Counseling: Problems and Methods
ROBERT MYRICK and JOE WITTMER

Secondary School Teaching: Problems and Methods
THEODORE W. HIPPLE

Solving Teaching Problems:
A Guide for the Elementary School Teacher
MILDRED BLUMING and MYRON H. DEMBO

Teaching, Loving, and Self-directed Learning
DAVID THATCHER

Will the Real Teacher Please Stand Up?
A Primer in Humanistic Education
MARY GREER and BONNIE RUBINSTEIN

SOLVING
TEACHING PROBLEMS
A GUIDE FOR THE
ELEMENTARY SCHOOL TEACHER

86005

Mildred Bluming
Los Angeles Unified School District

Myron H. Dembo
University of Southern California

GOODYEAR PUBLISHING COMPANY, INC.
Pacific Palisades, California

SOLVING TEACHING PROBLEMS: A GUIDE FOR THE ELEMENTARY
SCHOOL TEACHER by Mildred Bluming and Myron H. Dembo

Copyright © 1973
Goodyear Publishing Company, Inc.
Pacific Palisades, California

Current printing (last digit):

10 9 8 7 6 5 4 3 2 1

ISBN: 0-87620-037-4

Library of Congress Catalog Card Number: 72-93079

Y-0374-2

Printed in the United States of America

CONTENTS

PREFACE

Many books, both theoretical and practical, have been written for teachers—why, then, still another one?

We believe this book will be helpful in two ways—first, as a training manual for a problem-solving approach to teaching and, second, as a resource manual for identifying symptoms, possible causes, and solutions to classroom problems.

Many teachers, we have found, feel their own education was inadequate in preparing them for life in the classroom—for the hurly-burly, constant interactions and interruptions, and all the diverse behavior that a class of thirty or so students can produce. Moreover, we discovered, the teachers often found themselves so busy trying to cope with superficial symptoms—putting out fires, as it were—that they could not take the time to seek the causes. With this book, we hope, a teacher will be able to identify a symptom, look it up in the index, and discover its possible causes and possible ways of handling them.

To find the most obvious and recurring problems that plague teachers, we conducted a survey of teachers from schools with varying demographic factors, asking them to complete the statement, "My biggest problem in teaching is . . ." The completed statements plus our review of recent research studies on teaching problems guided us in determining which problems should be included in this book.

The most successful teachers are the most flexible teachers, Lefever (1967) states. But to be flexible, one must know the proven techniques, innovative ideas, and varied approaches that might be effective in any given situation. For the beginning teacher, we hope this book will provide him or her with a backlog of ideas to start with; for the experienced teacher, we hope it will replenish his grab bag of ideas needed during hectic times and perhaps give him new approaches to old problems.

The book is divided into four chapters. Chapter 1 describes a systematic approach to classroom problems by presenting a model for decision making. Chapter 2 describes symptoms that reveal possible causes of disruptive behavior, analyzes each cause, and develops several plans for dealing with the cause. Chapter 3 considers various plans for effective use of time—including ways of alleviating clerical fatigue, of saving student work from the wastebasket, and of dealing with one's personal aversion to parts of the curriculum he is required to teach. Chapter 4 discusses learning problems of the individual child and plans to enhance pupil learning—for example, how to keep precocious readers from being bored, what to do about children good in math but lagging in reading; this chapter also investigates individualized learning on a limited scale and pupil-team learning.

At the end of Chapters 2, 3, and 4 are several case incidents—accounts of classroom problems that may be used as exercises for problem solving—many of them based on real incidents observed by student teachers. Each case incident is followed by discussion questions and appropriate space for notes.

Our philosophy is this: there are no simple, instant answers to any problem, but we are obliged as teachers to keep trying to find answers. If a child's learning is being obstructed, faultfinding is not the answer. Thus, if our book helps teachers change from hand-wringers to seekers of solutions, it will have served the purpose for which we wrote it.

We would like to thank the many student teachers at the University of Southern California for providing us with ideas for the case incidents found in the book.

Mildred Bluming
Myron H. Dembo

SOLVING
TEACHING PROBLEMS

Chapter One

IMPROVING PROBLEM-SOLVING SKILLS

Few teachers leave their profession because they are untrained or unchallenged. However, many are discouraged by aggravations that interfere with normal teaching situations, and many find themselves unable to make effective decisions about the problems that arise in their classrooms.

"The biggest problem in the world," poet Witter Bynner wrote, "could have been solved when it was small," and teaching problems are no exception— particularly for teachers who try to wish problems away without doing anything about them.

In this first chapter we present an approach to classroom problem solving, using actual classroom incidents to illustrate its phases.

Consider the problem of Mrs. Parker, an experienced sixth-grade teacher who had difficulty initiating a new teaching strategy. At the suggestion of her new curriculum supervisor, she and the other intermediate-level teachers in her school tried, for the first time, a group-oriented inquiry approach to teaching social studies. During a one-day preschool workshop to discuss the new curriculum, Mrs. Parker reacted thus:

Mrs. Parker: I have thirty-five students this year, the most I've had in five years. I really feel that this new method will only waste time. These children can't work in groups! They'll be fooling around all the time!

Fellow Teacher: There are some excellent units on how to organize and work in groups in one of the supplementary language textbooks. Perhaps you could plan a few extra lessons on the topic?

Mrs. Parker: But when? If I spend time on that, I'll get behind in my language work. These children must understand grammar fully before they go on to junior high. If I don't start drilling now, I'll never get through all the material they are expected to know.

Fellow Teacher: Perhaps you could spend a few social studies periods before you start the first unit . . .

Mrs. Parker: But that would put us behind the other sixth grades in social studies. No, if we must try the new method, I'll start tomorrow. But I hope he [the curriculum supervisor] doesn't expect too much; there's only so much time in one day.

After giving one lecture to her class on the purpose and methods of working in groups, Mrs. Parker began the first unit in social studies by assigning students to different groups and giving each group a project to complete in three weeks. Few of the groups met the first week; during the second and third weeks some students worked diligently on their projects, but others did little. Finally when the groups held their last meetings to prepare their final presentations to the class, Mrs. Parker found the following. In two groups, members had nothing of value to report. In another, some sat sulking because one of their members left some vital material at home. In another, the four participants could not agree on the responsibility of the members. In a fourth group, one student refused to speak to the others. Faced with failure Mrs. Parker said, "That's the last time I try a new method I know won't work! That supervisor and his new methods!"

Another example of classroom problems occurred in a large urban school in which first-year teacher Miss Simpson, graduate of a highly selective women's college who had chosen the school because she wished to help disadvantaged children, was beginning with a fifth-grade class. During her third week Miss Simpson remarked to her principal that in college she had learned many techniques for teaching math and science, but none could be used with any of her students since, she said, "They can only concentrate for a short period of time and are very deficient in basic skills." The principal then asked whether her classroom procedures were appropriate for stimulating interest in these subjects. Miss Simpson explained how she always attempted to encourage her students to be well organized, assigned some homework daily, and allowed students to ask questions whenever they failed to understand her presentations.

After some discussion, the principal agreed to spend some time visiting the class to observe Miss Simpson's teaching and recommend possible solutions. One morning he observed her say to a student who had failed to complete his work, "Well, Robert, don't you think it's about time you started doing some work in this class?"

"I can't get anything done at my house," Robert replied. "With the television and radio always playing, it's too noisy."

Miss Simpson responded angrily: "I just don't know what to do! You people just will not try! Don't you have any pride in yourselves?"

In later visits the principal noticed that the class atmosphere was worsening, that the students responded less and less to Miss Simpson's questions, classroom work had dropped off, and Miss Simpson herself was growing more upset each day.

Mrs. Parker's and Miss Simpson's classroom situations are not unusual. They occur in many schools across the country. Yet these are only two of a great many troubling situations facing teachers, both beginning and experienced. But if nothing is done about these situations, the student's achievement, motivation, and social development may suffer.

Teachers approach problems in a variety of ways (as Schmuck *et al.*, 1966, point out). Some continually deny anything is wrong. Being too lazy to investigate a problem, they never look below the surface in any classroom situation. The child who suddenly seems no longer interested in school gets no special attention; the withdrawn child is given a seat in the back of the room and is not heard from again; the child who finishes his reading text before the end of the year is told to read the stories again. By denying the existence of possible problems, these teachers fantasize about the leisure of teaching and cannot understand how their colleagues can possibly have problems.

Other teachers operate as though they have a mandate from authority to handle all problems in a certain way—as exemplified by such comments as: "This is the way we do it at Parkview." Or, "My supervising teacher told me to handle all discipline problems this way." These teachers rely on school regulations, the principal's dictum, moral codes, or a set of customs for all decision making. They are very concerned with conformity and show little creativity in solving problems that cannot easily be handled by an established pattern of behavior.

A third kind of teacher solves problems with a superficial, "least-effort" style. He does not deny that problems exist, but he minimizes the time and energy that must be spent solving them—as represented by such comments as "I can have this class shaped up in no time," or "I'll find something for my advanced reading group to do to keep them busy." This teacher may try to explore academic or behavior problems if the needed resources are easily available, but if they are not, he may try a quick "patch-up" job.

A fourth approach is when teachers use their personal feelings or beliefs as the major criterion for their decisions. In gathering information about classroom problems, for instance, they will select that which conforms to their own personal frame of reference, often neglecting important data because they do not appear relevant. A teacher of this sort may be the first to blame parents of poverty children for all failure in school, pointing out to his colleagues, for example, that these parents do not regularly attend PTA meetings (forgetting that the parents may work, not have transportation, or feel uncomfortable about such meetings) and never investigating the possible reasons why because he has already made up his mind.

A fifth kind of teacher is overly empirical in approaching classroom problems. To this teacher, what he *sees* is the most important criterion in decision making. He pays little attention to students' underlying feelings or attitudes; rather, observations of classroom behavior always take priority.

Each of the above kinds of problem solving is faulty because it does not adequately use any logical approach to obtaining the facts or to developing a solution based on these facts. In the following pages we try to suggest a way in which decision making can be made a more logical and less emotional process. The model we shall follow consists of four important components of responsible decision making:

1. problem identification
2. diagnosis
3. plan development
4. evaluation.

Many expert problem solvers, such as physicians and psychiatrists, use this model or some close facsimile in approaching problems. We could have presented other models, but we believe this one is simple yet meaningful enough to help alleviate many of the faulty approaches to problem solving discussed above. As Figure 1 shows, the model is cyclical, since in some cases one finds that after he has evaluated a plan he has not solved the problem and must therefore try to reidentify it.

Let us now examine each phase of the model.

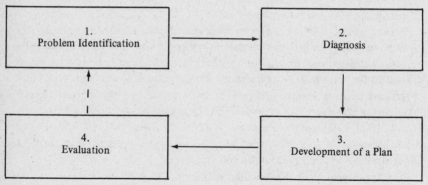

Figure 1. The four phases of the problem-solving sequence

PROBLEM IDENTIFICATION

In the first phase of problem solving, we must have a concise understanding of the situation. Mrs. Parker had a problem that was easily identifiable; she was well aware, in fact, that inquiry teaching was her nemesis. Miss Simpson's problem, however, was less obvious—and most classroom problems fall into this category.

The importance of clearly understanding the nature of a problem cannot be overestimated. It is not uncommon to hear a teacher state, "There is something wrong with my class, but I can't quite put my finger on it," or "For some reason, I can't get any work out of my class this week." Such statements are a start toward identifying a problem, but one's conceptualization of it cannot stop here: unless one tries to formulate some finer assumptions about the nature of the problem, he will never reach the three remaining problem-solving phases.

Classroom problems take many forms, and some are perennial thorns—especially problems of motivation, discipline, and instructional planning. How can Jim be encouraged to complete his assignments? How can Susan be kept from interrupting other students during class? How can students be grouped according to ability if doing so means developing three different lesson plans? All teachers are faced with such problems, and thus should be thinking about some general approaches to them.

Some problems must be handled immediately, others after the teacher has had some time to study them. Obviously, a sudden outburst in class which finds two students in a fight must be dealt with promptly. But if the problem is complex and on-going, the teacher has time to consider future responses. The deteriorating work of a student, for example, is a problem that can be studied over a period of time without requiring immediate action. Hopefully, as a teacher becomes more skilled in handling this kind of problem, his spur-of-the-moment decisions should also improve. One advantage of the experienced teacher is that he is better able than the inexperienced teacher to anticipate the results of his actions in particular situations, and thus he is more likely to select a more effective response from among his options.

Some types of behavior are more easily identifiable—that of an aggressive or belligerent pupil, for instance—because they come into direct conflict with the teacher's instructional goals. But a withdrawn pupil, though he may be less a threat to the teacher, may have a more serious personality problem than his aggressive peer. It is important that the teacher carefully observe individual students during classroom activities. The insightful book *How Children Fail* (Holt, 1964, p. 21) reminds us that "you can't find out what a child does in class by looking at him only when he is called on. You have to watch him for long stretches of time without his knowing it."

Other problems cannot be studied without analyzing classroom peer relations. Often the learning process is enhanced or inhibited by the kinds of relations students have with each other during the class, the type of norms established. For example, in some classrooms, helping other students is appropriate behavior; in others it is not. We recall one fifth-grade student, working in a team with three other students to solve some mathematics problems, who hid her paper after completing the assignment. Asked why she was not helping the other students, she answered: "Because they might catch up with me." The reason was that this student was one of the better math students in the class, and she believed that if she helped other students her ranking would be endangered.

It is essential that the teacher determine the type of peer relations that dominate the class. Are students generally friendly, or aggressive or hostile? Are there many popular students or only a few? Are some students isolated or rejected? Are some dominating class discussions and decision making? Are cliques interfering with cooperative classroom activities? The answers to these questions can often help a teacher identify a problem related to group behavior (Schmuck *et al.*, 1966).

Many classroom problems are related to the teacher's own personality and teaching style. These problems are often manifested in how he relates to his students and how he organizes his lesson plans and conducts class activities. Because the teacher is least likely to attribute classroom difficulties to his own behavior, he may find it difficult to identify problems in this category. This is an important area, as reflected by recent research (such as that of Brophy and Good, 1970) on how teacher behavior affects student behavior. The following are questions to ask about this relationship: Does my attitude toward a particular subject influence my students' interest in that subject? Do my verbal attacks on certain students have any effect on the others? Do the type of questions I ask influence the level of my students' thinking? Do I talk too much?

DIAGNOSIS

After one thinks he has identified a problem, he must then probe beneath the surface to refute or confirm his assumptions. The guiding question to ask here is: Why did the behavior occur? By trying to answer it, one moves to a higher level of generalization.

Another purpose of this diagnosis phase is to integrate all the derivative problems you noticed in the first phase so that they can be dealt with together rather than separately (Schmuck *et al.,* 1966). This organization is extremely important because any primary problem usually has numerous derivative problems. For example, Mrs. Parker's difficulty with the inquiry approach to teaching social studies also led to discipline and motivational problems. With careful diagnosis it is less likely the teacher will have to treat each of these derivative problems individually.

Many teachers neglect this phase and move directly to the development of a plan after they have identified a problem. The danger of not carefully diagnosing a problem is that the teacher may misinterpret its true nature and attempt a premature and incorrect solution.

The diagnosis of a problem should relate to the identification of the problem. In other words, if you were to identify a behavior problem related to the home environment of a particular student, you would attempt to obtain information about the home environment via parent interviews, questionnaires, or home visitations. You would be less likely to diagnose the total problem by simply studying the child's reading scores or observing his behavior during class. A good point to remember is to try to follow all inferences in Phase One with objective behavioral data. This will help maintain a direct relationship between problem identification and diagnosis.

The work during diagnosis is like the work of a lawyer in that one tries to build a case by supporting all contentions with behavioral and empirical evidence. How does a teacher collect evidence? The procedures vary according to the problem, but there are general methods of gathering data. One is by observing classroom behavior, with the teacher trying to make his observations as objective as possible. Of course a teacher has his biases, values, and attitudes, which interfere with his objectivity, so that he must continually ask himself, for example, "Did Bill really hit Mike or did I blame Bill because I have been upset with his classroom behavior?" (Greenwood *et al.*, 1971).

There are numerous diagnostic aids that one can use with little training which measure social relations, classroom norms, interests, and attitudes. Most teacher training courses describe such assessment devices as *sociometry,* the study of social relations; *sentence completion tests,* which provide information about students' interests, feelings, and attitudes; and the widely used *Flanders Interaction Analysis system* (described in many sources—see Amidon and Flanders, 1967; Amidon and Hough, 1968; White, 1969) by which the teacher may analyze his own classroom behavior and collect data about important aspects in pupil-teacher interaction (for example: Do I do too much of the talking in the classroom? How much time do I spend in lecturing? Do I spend enough time in the extension of student ideas?).

A list of useful references for problem solving is provided at the end of this book; however, two particularly helpful sources should be mentioned here: *Diagnosing Classroom Learning Environments* (Fox *et al.*, 1966), which provides useful questionnaire-type instruments for measuring all aspects of classroom dynamics, and *Ways of Studying Children* (Almy, 1959), which emphasizes observational techniques during classroom activities.

Research studies and descriptions of innovative programs published in educational journals can also help with diagnosis as well as plan development. For example, the question whether verbal punishment of certain students will affect the remaining students in class could be answered by articles by Kounin and Gump (1958, 1961), who found that a teacher's bad temper in handling misbehavior disturbed the whole class, not just the pupils criticized, and that a punitive teacher's scoldings made the entire class more aggressive. Of course, not every educational problem can be as easily solved, but research studies can often provide insights for better understanding problems. To test your skill at this kind of data collection, ask yourself whether you know how to read a research article, know which educational journals are most helpful to your work, and know how to locate appropriate reference material in a library. If you lack some of these skills, your effectiveness as a problem solver may be diminished.

Lastly, don't forget the educational psychology, sociology, and methods courses you are taking or have taken. Theories and principles that might have appeared useless at one time may be helpful in understanding present problems: for example, reinforcement theory (Clarizio, 1971) might be used to analyze poor student-teacher relationships, or Maslow's (1970) hierarchical theory of motivation to analyze why poverty children often cannot concentrate on their studies. Social science courses can help one understand the causes and motivation behind human behavior, in making sense out of seemingly random behavior.

A teacher usually has his own theory about why certain behavior occurs; it is important he properly investigate its validity by collecting data to confirm or refute it. How he goes about this task during the diagnosis phase can also influence his success as a problem solver.

DEVELOPMENT OF A PLAN

In this phase, all the information obtained during the diagnosis phase is pulled together into a logical plan to solve the problem. The plan should be broad enough to handle most of the derivative problems associated with the major problem. For example, for Mrs. Parker the plan should allow her to use inquiry teaching while at the same time alleviate the disciplinary and motivational problems associated with her use of group activities.

The various aspects of the plan and the diagnosis should be consistent, for if the plan is not directly related to the diagnosis it probably will not solve the problem. For example, if Miss Simpson's principal diagnosed her problem as being insufficient instructional planning to develop interesting class presentations, then a proper plan would be to increase the time spent in preparation or to change her teaching strategy. However, if her problem is caused by a lack of understanding of children from the culture of poverty, increased preparation time would be of little help.

Plans should be developed which are feasible in the particular school situation to which they will be applied (Greenwood *et al.,* 1971), and should take into account such factors as demands on teacher time, available resources, and individual abilities. For example, a teacher might want to visit his students' homes in order to better understand how their home environments influence their classroom behavior; however, such visits would be extremely time consuming for any teacher. Or a teacher might want to obtain a second set of reading texts for students who complete their assigned material early; however, a school district might not be able to afford a second set of books. One must always ask: Is the plan feasible in the context of the situation being analyzed?

A plan must also be operational; the teacher must be able to translate his decision into the specific procedures he (or others) will perform (Greenwood *et al.,* 1971). For example, a teacher may decide to handle a particular child's discipline problem by "meeting him on his own level," but what are the specific procedures for doing this? individualized reading assignments? showing interest in his hobbies? To check whether a plan is operational, try describing it to someone else to see if he also could carry it out. This test also illustrates the importance of teachers working together to solve problems. Often teachers believe no one else in the school has the same teaching problems, and they are reluctant to discuss their problems with colleagues for fear of appearing incompetent. Much could be gained if teachers shared innovative teaching ideas that had helped them with their problems. In fact, time can be set aside each week or month for problem-solving activities during meetings or conferences.

EVALUATION

In this, the last phase of problem solving, the essential question is whether the plan is working. If it does not change behavior and solve the problem, it must be modified or discarded. The teacher should then retrace his steps from the identification stage to determine where errors have occurred—particularly, misinterpretation of behavior, faulty data collection, and poor plan development. "Try, try again" is particularly relevant to the problem-solving model. One teacher who did *not* try to reidentify the problem found herself keeping the "class clown" for weeks after school as punishment for disrupting the class, yet the student still did not modify his behavior; but the teacher did not change her approach to the problem because she still considered the student a "wise guy" and never further analyzed his behavior. There are many other lingering classroom problems which consistently irritate many teachers, but they are not solved because the teachers fail to take other approaches to the problems.

There are many ways in which the teacher can obtain feedback to evaluate the success of a new teaching strategy, style, or method. Diagnostic aids administered during the diagnosis phase may be given again in the evaluation phase as posttests. For example, if a teacher was concerned with student hostility and administered a sociometric test to determine how well the students liked each other, he could readminister the test after implementing a plan in order to assess his plan's effectiveness. If the test showed a reduction in isolated and neglected children, a more equal distribution of popularity among students, the teacher could call his plan successful.

Other ways to obtain feedback are through group and individual discussions with students in the class. Students are usually honest in their reactions when the teacher provides an environment in which they do not feel threatened. Evaluation can also be obtained by asking fellow teachers to observe a class, thus allowing the teacher to ask pertinent questions about particular aspects of his behavior. Do not forget also the use of the tape recorder, with which one can evaluate his instruction at his own convenience and play back specific incidents for further study.

Let us now return to the two teaching problems presented earlier to learn how they were resolved, following the outline of the problem-solving process.

MRS. PARKER'S CLASSROOM

Problem identification

Mrs. Parker had difficulty using the new group inquiry approach to teaching social studies suggested by her curriculum supervisor. As a result, the following derivative problems occurred: a) increased discipline worries, b) incomplete assignments, and c) development of hostile student attitudes toward group work and each other.

Diagnosis

Mrs. Parker realized that the major cause of her problem was her lack of preparation for group instruction. The one brief lecture she heard on the purpose and methods of working in groups was insufficient at the start of a new learning experience. Pressured for time, she went ahead without adequately planning her work or preparing her students.

Development of a plan

Mrs. Parker suggested to the curriculum supervisor that he schedule additional meetings with teachers using the same method to discuss mutual problems and exchange ideas. He agreed, since other teachers were expressing some of the same problems. From these meetings, Mrs. Parker implemented the following ideas:

a) Students were organized into groups of four and were requested to role-play a situation in which a group had a bossy chairman, one in which a student didn't want to work with others in the group, and another in which a student didn't want to assume any responsibility. Students were also asked to discuss ways in which they might effectively deal with such behavior.

b) She prepared small study guides for each group to help in group organization and to provide some structure for the completion of the assignments. Included in the guides were reference material, a list of responsibilities which had to be assigned, and suggestions for proper note taking, outlining, and preparation of reports.

c) Instead of leaving the students completely on their own as she had done earlier, Mrs. Parker changed her role to that of a coordinator and consultant. Although she was not a discussion leader, she moved from group to group looking for potential questions and problems. When asked a question, she did not attempt to take over by laying out all the steps necessary for its solution but instead encouraged the group members to help each other solve the problem.

During the teacher meetings, it was decided that the teachers should engage in the inquiry process by finding appropriate journal articles or research studies related to group learning in social studies. Many teachers found useful articles in *Social Education,* a periodical devoted to social studies education. Another teacher found the book *Classroom Group Behavior* by Bany and Johnson (1964) helpful because it provided accounts of research studies related to group dynamics as well as suggestions for improving group behavior in any situation. Mrs. Parker herself found some interesting articles in group cohesiveness which convinced her that she should give more attention to the manner of formulating groups. In particular, she found research studies reported by Lott and Lott

(1960; 1961) meaningful. They reported that better individual learning takes place in high-cohesive than in low-cohesive groups (other things being equal); that is, individuals in the presence of highly liked others perform better on learning tasks than individuals in the presence of less liked others. Although Mrs. Parker realized that the Lott and Lott research situations were not totally similar to her classroom situation, she still found them pertinent. She decided, therefore, to use a sociometric instrument to ascertain the liking patterns of her students so that she could formulate more effective groups.

Evaluation

After the adaption of the above plan, each teacher decided to keep an anecdotal record of the problems still unsolved. Weekly meetings were held to diagnose and develop solutions to meet these problems.

In her class, Mrs. Parker asked each student group to select a chairman to report to the class the group's opinions of the new changes in procedure. Although there were still remarks about individual students not doing their work plus some minor procedural problems, the groups reported much greater cooperation among participants than had existed earlier. They also reported that the most helpful innovation was the study guides.

Mrs. Parker kept a daily account of behavior problems throughout this period. She noted a sharp decrease in discipline problems, which substantiated the groups' findings that their members had become more cooperative after the changes in classroom procedures.

MISS SIMPSON'S CLASSROOM

Problem identification

Miss Simpson was unable to communicate effectively with students from low socioeconomic backgrounds. This lack of rapport influenced her teaching so that she often failed to motivate students and maintain their interest during class sessions.

Diagnosis

Miss Simpson's principal observed three specific instances of this lack of communication:

a) She lectured a student for not caring and not having enough pride in his accomplishments—assumptions lacking supportive evidence.
b) She did not appear to understand the student's comment that he had no place to study at home, for she failed to explore the situation further.
c) Whenever a student gave an incorrect answer, she corrected him immediately. She seemed to respond positively only to correct answers.

The principal believed that Miss Simpson should try to determine the attitude of her students toward class instruction. He suggested that she use an instrument which the class could respond to twice: the first time they would describe how they felt, the second time how they thought the teacher felt about the same concerns. Part of the instrument is shown in Figure 2 (Armstrong *et al.,* 1970). Miss Simpson agreed to try the technique.

A. How I feel B. How my teacher feels	Agree most of the time	Agree more than disagree	Agree as much as disagree	Disagree more than agree	Disagree most of the time
Students should ask for extra help from the teacher if they need it					
Students should tell the teacher when they don't understand some material					
Students should finish homework assignment each day					

Figure 2. Attitude instrument. The student may express answers to A and B in each blank. Or he may receive two forms—"How I feel" and "How my teacher feels."

Source: Adapted from Robert Armstrong et al., *The Development and Evaluation of Behavioral Objects* (Worthington, Ohio: Charles A. Jones, 1970), p. 70. Reprinted by permission of the authors and the publisher

For each statement in the left-hand column the students checked one column (from Agree to Disagree) which best represented their attitudes. Each of the response categories was assigned a value (1 through 5); total responses of the pupils in each column were multiplied by the appropriate value to determine a total class attitude. Using this device, the principal was able to show Miss Simpson how the students' attitudes differed from their perception of their teacher's attitude about important classroom procedures. Most of the class, for example, disagreed that "students should tell the teacher when they don't understand some material"—a particularly distressing finding to Miss Simpson since she believed the class understood she was willing to help them. The principal pointed out that the students indeed understood this (as their responses showed) but still concluded asking for help was not a good idea, and that one reason, perhaps, was that Miss Simpson tended to be "right-answer oriented" and appeared to show displeasure with incorrect answers. He asked Miss Simpson whether students could learn as much from incorrect as from correct answers and discussed additional discrepancies in the attitude instrument.

Development of a plan

The principal suggested that Miss Simpson try the following:
a) Familiarize herself with her students' neighborhoods by driving through

them and stopping at the shopping district and whenever possible visiting the homes of students.

b) Contact the school social worker or counselor to learn more about the backgrounds of the students.

c) Allow the students to use her room after school to complete homework assignments.

d) Participate in some extracurricular activity (for example, sponsoring a science club), thus making herself available for more personal contact with students in a nonacademic atmosphere.

e) Use more positive reinforcement in class.

f) Vary instructional procedures and not spend the whole period lecturing.

g) Lastly, read McCandless's *Children: Behavior and Development* (1967), especially the chapter "Middle Class Teacher and Every Class Child," which discusses the differences in values.

Evaluation

After a few weeks the principal observed that more students were asking questions and participating in class discussions and that the number of reprimands by Miss Simpson had decreased.

Miss Simpson reported that by studying her students' backgrounds she had become more aware of possible reasons for certain learning problems and was also better equipped to deal with behavior problems. Two months after the plan's inception, the students were given the same attitude instruments, which this time showed a greater congruence between the students' attitude and their perception of Miss Simpson's attitude.

In the problems discussed, different approaches could have been taken to solving them. Were the diagnosis and the plan consistent? Were the plans feasible and operational? If you had the same problems, would you have used the same diagnostic instrument and the same evaluation procedure?

In the next three chapters we shall deal with three broad teaching problems: discipline, effective use of time, and organizing for learning. Other areas could also be discussed, but these three are most frequently mentioned by teachers. We shall attempt to relate each of these problem areas to the model described here. That is, each chapter begins with the *identification* of specific problems related to the topic, then raises questions related to *diagnosis* and *plan development*—for example: Have you investigated possible reasons for lack of respect? Has respect been earned? (diagnosis). Have you tried these approaches? (plan development). In some cases, the diagnosis and plan development discussion cover both with a single question. Finally, short case incidents involve the reader in the problem-solving process. We suggest these incidents be discussed in class or with colleagues along with other incidents emerging from your own observation or teaching experience. In many cases, library research will be helpful in gathering information to deal with discussion questions.

Chapter Two

DISRUPTIVE BEHAVIOR PROBLEMS

CLASSROOM CONTROL

A new teacher usually approaches his first teaching assignment with extreme trepidation and exalted idealism. Such anxiety can create feelings of inadequacy, and the idealistic aspirations, if unrealized, can lead to great disappointment. After failing to cope with a classroom full of active youngsters trying to test the limits of their new teacher, one might begin to doubt his ability to teach. At this point, the best course is to ask the kind of questions that might help diagnose the problems that usually plague a beginning teacher.

(1) Have you looked and listened for clues that will help you diagnose the problem of a particular child?

Many teachers limit their cumulative card investigations to the curriculum area. At the start of each semester a teacher is given a cumulative record card for each child. On it is recorded information about family, data from both group and individual tests, curriculum to which he has been exposed, and, finally, short comments from previous teachers.

Knowing that a teacher's expectations can affect a pupil's performance, many teachers limit their cumulative card investigations to the curriculum area. Their reason for not looking at a previous teacher's comments is that they do not want to approach a child with someone else's opinion or expectation. (See Rosenthal and Jacobson, 1968, for a discussion of the possible effects of teacher expectation on pupil performance.) They prefer to make decisions based on their own experience with a pupil. Recent studies indicate that it might be advisable for teachers to form some personal opinions about a pupil's work before investigating previous performance (Brophy and Good, 1970; Good, 1970).

The family history can be noted, but it is most important to elicit this information from the child himself through questionnaires or completion of incomplete sentences. Primary school children can dictate their stories of their families to you while you type them. Or you can have them write these histories as an exercise in creative writing. The information on the cumulative card is given by the adult who registered the child, whereas the stories children tell or write are their own perceptions of their position in the family.

A child may misread the actions of his parents or siblings which can be the nucleus of a future emotional problem. Thus, an important clue for you is how the child sees himself. The noted semanticist S. I. Hayakawa once stated that he could not understand why mountain climbers tackled the most treacherous mountains, since many died as a result—until he discovered that they climbed a mountain not only because it was there but also because they had a *self-image* of being mountain climbers. Hayakawa also gave the example of an English literature expert who considered himself a specialist on Thackeray. If someone were to ask him a question about Thackeray, and if he did not know the answer, he would surely look it up at the very first opportunity. In his mind he was a *specialist* in that subject and therefore should know all there was to know; consequently, no one had to remind him to look for the answer to that question. The child's self-image can be a powerful ally or a detrimental troublemaker for both the child and the group in which he finds himself.

Listen to children's problems. Once in a while, have a short group-therapy period by taking a few minutes' time in the morning. For example, begin with the thought-provoking topic of fear, which is very relevant to children. What frightens them? Role playing to help solve someone's problem can be done throughout a child's school career. Helping children realize that no one answer is the right answer for all problems (nor for all people) can aid them in avoiding the habit of reacting automatically without thinking. Sessions should be of short duration and are to be devoted to talk from children, not sermons from you. Call on children individually and ask them if they agree with another child's answer. Ask the question "why" very often.

Notice extreme reactions to seemingly innocent incidents. Such a case occurred when Mrs. Walters distributed an arithmetic worksheet to one of her math groups. The students had been well prepared to work independently on particular problems, yet as she turned to her other group to start a teacher-directed skill lesson, she noticed Jim was slashing at his paper with his pencil in a scribble-like pattern. Scolding Jim for his behavior would have been a useless response to such an obviously nonverbal cry for help. Mrs. Walters thought it might be a feeling of frustration that caused Jim's reaction, but at that moment she did not have time to investigate the source of the problem. She told Jim he would be helped with his paper at a later time and asked him to be her assistant while she taught the other group. In this way she avoided a disruptive experience for the whole class and prepared the way for a productive conference with Jim at a later time. The important aim of her actions was to build a spirit of cooperation that would help her in identifying, diagnosing, and planning to help him solve his problem.

Let children express their feelings. Why not have a pet-peeve box and a suggestion box into which children can put their gripes (Blackham, 1968)? It can be a very revealing feedback device that will aid you in pinpointing a probable cause of a classroom problem. Instead of discussing complaints that have been elicited from children with the whole group, why not have several committees take the problem under advisement? Solutions can be very different and efficacious at the same time.

The use of questionnaires is another source of feedback for you that can be of inestimable help in making education relevant for the children in your class. There are many different areas you can investigate by using this method. Fox *et al.* (1966) discuss relevant questions which you also might ask on aspects of classroom life.

(2) Are you aware how much your behavior contributes to the classroom environment?

Your behavior, to a great extent, influences and evokes responses from your students. Think of how you react to a smile and a friendly greeting. What is your reaction to a dour and frowning face? This type of confrontation often brings out hostility in adults and usually does so in children because they think your frown means disapproval of them. Adults will try to terminate unpleasant contacts as soon as possible, but students are captives—in fact, Jackson (1968) compares them to prisoners held captive in an institution. Since your students cannot turn away from you physically (at least most of the time), they use other methods to get even with the grumpy person who has made them feel uncomfortable and unsettled. If your students are not at peace with themselves, your classroom will not be a peaceful one.

Since you are not an automaton who is always happy, energetic, and smiling, you may find it necessary to pretend you are "on stage." Many times you will find yourself giving a performance that is worthy of an Oscar. However, if you are not a good actor, what is wrong with a short group discussion with your students? Discussions about what makes you feel grumpy can help children verbalize some of their frustrations and may help you in your role as a diagnostician. An informal opener for the discussion might be: "What makes your day start wrong?" Without going into personal details, one can talk about not getting enough sleep. You can discuss how someone else's "mad" started you on that unrewarding path to grouchiness. Not feeling quite right physically, having a headache, perhaps, or an upset stomach, is another cause to explore. It is discussions such as these that help children verbalize some of their problems. Students can be led to understand that it is not always their fault that a day does not go as it should.

Have you a good way to channel your anger or of working out personal frustrations? Why not share it with your class? This type of discussion is worthy of time in the classroom. Think of the mental health implications and citizenship training that can be acomplished.

Have you a sense of humor? Share a good laugh with your students by the use of funny riddles (as brainteasers), which can be found in books. You might start the day with them and provide the answer to a particular riddle at the end of the day.

When you discuss a child's work, make him aware that you understand any difficulty he might be having. Talk about an experience you had as a child and how you might have struggled with some aspect of the curriculum. It is very encouraging to a youngster who is having difficulty to hear about the ultimate success of one who had a similar problem. This is especially true if it is the teacher who had a learning problem.

Most children take a great delight in having the teacher become one of them. Sometimes eat lunch with your students or spend an informal hour in conversations. You might be surprised at the differences you will notice in how children react to you. Participate in their baseball, handball, or jump-rope games. All of these humanizing activities show students you care about them as people rather than just as pupils in the classroom. Sell yourself as a human being, a caring one, and if they buy this, there is a strong possibility they will try to live up to your highest expectations.

(3) Do you think of children as responsible people who can help plan and evaluate?

This attitude creates relevant education for the children. They become full partners, have a share in this business of learning, and therefore have a personal interest in what they are doing. If students are interested, they become inner-motivated and need no outer imposed control. If children are permitted to evaluate, they are helped to learn to judge for themselves. As Glasser (1969, p. 38) wrote, "the process of stating the problem, finding reasonable alternatives, and implementing what seems to be the best alternative, is education." This is learning that should begin in the kindergarten, in more simple ways, and continue through all stages of education.

Critical thinking helps us out of many troubling situations. McDonald and Nelson (1955) illustrate this point with the following example: If two children who are having an argument come to you, each one insisting that he was wronged or was set upon first, you can make them responsible for finding the solution. You can explain that since you were not there when the action took place, perhaps they can get together and try to find a solution to their problem. You are the teacher but you cannot be the judge in this case. Something obviously happened; can they think it through and come up with some answers that will solve this dilemma? Watch the way two solons get down to cases.

Evaluation by the children at different times of the day, especially at the end of the day, helps students become efficient in upholding standards that are useful, in becoming aware of what your goals are, and what they should strive for. If, for example, they were not successful with a rule that had been decided upon by all, help them learn the value of asking why a decision made by all did not work. The group does not have to be nagged about the breakdown of the rule. They have to try to discover what went wrong. Was the regulation too unrealistic? Did they fully understand what was required of them? Have they the ability to follow through? In doing this you are helping them become problem solvers. If children are not given help in this area, they tend to evade problems, lie about situations to get out of them, depend on others to solve their problems for them, or just give up. Rather than be the omnipotent judge who tells them they have acted wrongly and must not do it again, help them make discoveries by themselves. Dreikurs (1968, p. 81) stated that part of today's social upheavals can be traced to the fact that "we underestimate greatly the ability of children, their intelligence, and their capacity for responsibility."

(4) Are there unusual circumstances that are creating restlessness in the children?

Excitement is communicative. A windy day, the day before vacation, preparations for a program performance, a rainy day—all of these are perfectly valid reasons for hyperactivity and fast reactions. Prepare for such days. Put your ready-made plans away, if need be, and substitute a relaxed program. Give longer blocks of time to art, story telling, creative writing. Instead of the usual reading, have a language-experience reading lesson (discussed later) or start a story and have someone add a word until the story is finished. Ask for the biggest and most unheard-of lie, tale, or excuse to get out of doing a chore or homework. Booklets can be made up of this story and then read aloud in small groupings.

Instead of the usual math lesson, ask the children to measure closets, tables, charts, with string, rolls of adding-machine paper, or any other unusual measuring device. They can compare results by having two teams measure the same thing but use different kinds of measuring materials; it is the same area, but different answers are correct.

With some children a written assignment seems to have a quieting effect. If possible there should be a reason for this work, so that it is not just busy work from which they cannot benefit. For example, to make students aware of the types of sentences that use different punctuation marks, ask them to write examples of sentences that use a question mark, an exclamation point, quotation marks, and parentheses. Many children enjoy classification work. Tell them to find zoo animals in their picture dictionary, or in the regular dictionary, if they are in the upper grades. There are many classifications that can be used—farm animals, workers who come to their homes, furniture, parts of a building, and so forth.

Have small groups and let one person read to each group. A slow reader working with an even slower group is greatly motivated to read more and more. This type of team learning is a wonderful morale booster to those who might have given up trying to compete.

In all of these activities there will be many incidental learnings going on. It is not important to have subjects at their regular times. Reorganize the activities of the day. There will be learning going on but in a way that will help your students forget, or help them control, that feeling of suppressed excitement or the butterflies in their stomachs. Keep them occupied doing the kind of fun things they enjoy.

Have a do-it-again box that contains seat work the children have already had. Any extra seat work for your class can be filed in this box. When children have finished their current assignment, they can go to this box and choose work they had done some time ago. It gives them a feeling of accomplishment to discover that the work they once thought hard to do seems very easy now.

Have simple crossword puzzles available. Even the first-grade children can be taught this skill. Once the children grasp the concept of the puzzles, they enjoy them very much.

Let them play Concentration. They can use a deck of twenty teacher-made cards on which are written words they might need to review. Each word is printed on two cards. After the cards have been shuffled the child places them face down on the table, putting five cards across and four down. The first player turns over two randomly chosen cards. If they match, he takes them; if they do not match, he turns them face down again, and the next player gets his turn. The game is not only fun but also induces a great deal of learning in an informal manner. You can also use math combinations on these cards, having an equation on one card and the answer on another. For the young child use shapes, letters, and pictures.

Do not be afraid of using unconventional ideas. Play both rock and classical records. Have the students discuss what the music makes them think about, how it makes them feel. Let them express themselves rhythmically by using pencils or chopsticks to beat out the rhythm.

The point here is that you can help relieve the students' inner tensions by suiting the program to them. If your program is not fitting their moods, it is not efficient, and most likely it will not bring about the desired instructional objectives. Do not try to force your will on the children. There is always the possibility that you will lose—not only the program you wanted to use, but the desire of the children to please you.

(5) Do you have plans for the day?

To hold the interest of an audience, a director makes detailed plans before the play's rehearsals. His objective is to guide the actors to elicit the best performance they can give. He makes use of stage settings to create effects that highlight certain actions and subordinate others.

Likewise, teachers too have scripts—namely, their manuals. You should be aware of the importance of setting the stage for learning and the advance planning that is needed to prepare the varied approaches your students will need to operate at their maximum potential. If you haphazardly make last-minute assignments that are irrelevant to the needs and abilities of your pupils, you are setting the stage for loss of classroom control. Students who lose interest in their work will look around for more satisfying ways to fill their time and will create their own interest along lines that can lead to contagious chaos. Children become the directors of the activity because you have not set the stage for the kind of learning that will involve them and absorb their interest.

Once you accept the idea that planning is necessary for effective teaching, you should choose the method of planning that best suits you, your students, and your program. For example, if you are working in an individualized program, plans are made cooperatively with your student during the time in which you are having a conference with him. Some of your preplanning should concentrate on the learning centers (see Chap. 4) that are used to reinforce certain skills you have taught. Other plans should be made for the areas in which you will teach larger groups. For the traditional classroom program, some teachers have found that Monday afternoon is the best time to plan a weekly program. This helps them avoid a weekend lapse of memory, so that when they come in Monday morning they do not have to spend precious time trying to remember what happened the previous Friday afternoon. Also, teachers are often in a hurry to leave school on Friday afternoons and rarely think of making plans for the following week. If they become ill during the weekend and have not left any lesson plans, the substitute is forced to try to learn what they have been doing from the students and is thus apt to become more confused than enlightened. This situation creates a chaotic room and is one of the causes of the "on-vacation" feeling children get when their teacher is absent.

Some teachers prefer semiweekly planning of smaller units of learning. Others are happiest planning a daily program at the end of each school day, although they must be sure to keep in mind the overall picture of their long-term objectives as well as their immediate aims. Plans can be short, simple, and loosely outlined, or minutely detailed. Beginning teachers find it helps to know what they are going to do in detail. As they become more experienced and get to know their students better, they can then use the simpler forms.

Your plans should give you an idea of what you are going to cover in each subject area. At the end of each day, or at recess time, take a few minutes to evaluate what you have accomplished and, if needed, revise the following day's plans. These quick checks can be done at odd moments of the day and are necessary because there are times when you will gain new insights and perceive a possible cause of a learning problem. If you note this change immediately in your lesson plans, then your future plans can be revised and your objectives can be made more relevant to your students. In this manner you may avoid some of the unexpected situations that arise every day.

If a plan you have presented proves unsuitable and your students show a lack of interest for one reason or another, it is often best to stop the activity and involve the group in something that will interest them. When you are standing in the front of the room you will be able to tell whether the majority of your pupils are restless, fidgety, or daydreaming. Have a mental grab bag of ideas from which you can draw a novelty that will capture their attention. A word game that can spark up a group is that of naming a state that begins with the final letter of a previously named state. One can use countries, names of people, or food as subjects to be named. (For more games see Tredt and Tredt, 1965.) Always pull your group together before trying to teach anything. Just as an adult can shut off the TV when a program is boring him, children can tune out the on-going classroom activity. Unfortunately, you cannot always tell who has tuned out; but if the majority are sending out inattention signals, get ready to shift.

(6) Have you checked out the audiovisual equipment you will need?

Knowing your AV equipment—filmstrip projectors, movie projectors, and listening centers—is an important part of preplanning. When you have motivated your students and have created a mental set to learn, any interruption will cause a vacuum that will be immediately filled by restlessness and talk on the part of your students. You have motivated them and they are ready to move on, but must mark time until something has to be fixed or a new machine has to be borrowed. Make sure you have machines that are operable and ready for use. If you do this checking out before your group assembles, you will have time to replace or fix whatever is wrong.

(7) Are all the other needed materials at hand?

An awkward pause while you rummage for materials is an open invitation for children to lose the continuity of thought that you have been building. You lose valuable momentum, and the flow from motivation to learning is interrupted. Instead of fruitful learning, the children turn their attention to activities that are not among your stated objectives.

One way to avoid these disruptive periods is to have a subject-matter file that you organize every morning or the previous afternoon. Behind each subject are the papers that children will need for written and independent work. In this file you can put the books you will need or any other materials that you have prepared for that day's use. This is also a good place to file the folder with reminders to yourself of the various duties that you are responsible for. If you become aware of the need for a visual aid that might clarify a concept for the children, write yourself a note to that effect. This will obviate the agonizing need of trying to remember something and not being able to recall exactly what that something was. Thoughts that are vivid in the face of need might fade into forgetfulness during a busy day. At the end of the day check the file of things to be done. You will be surprised about how many you forgot completely.

(8) Have you organized your program so that the children can work independently?

Loss of group control is not so much caused by a student's emotional problem as by a lack of skill by the teacher; he has failed to organize the daily program in a way that meets the individual needs of the children and the requirements of the group (Blackham, 1968). Routines and duties should be established both by you and your students; they should be worked on consistently because standards and rules for group living are taught, not inherited. Good organization is accomplished when each person in the group knows what to do, because people work best with others when they know what is expected of them. Since forgetfulness is a trait of children no less than adults, they must be reminded of what is expected of them in a consistent manner.

Take time at the very beginning of the semester to teach your students how to operate machines they will be using. In all grades, including the primary ones, children can be trained to handle record players, to run filmstrip projectors, and how to turn tape recorders on and off. For the very young you can use a red piece of colored tape for the "stop" button and a green piece for the "go" button. Teach them how to dismantle listening centers and set them up; they can do it very neatly if taught how. Each child can be given an opportunity to show you how he handles the machine; if he does it well, award him an operating card that certifies he has mastered the skill. This check of machine skills can be done while the rest of the class is engaged in an independent activity. In the middle and upper elementary grades, a competent student can be used to check out those who have mastered the necessary skills.

Have interesting learning centers around the periphery of the room where children can work independently when they are finished with their individual assignments. Number these centers, and post charts that show the children which centers are available for their use at this time. (This procedure is discussed in detail in Chap. 4.) Remember to limit the number of participants at each center, because some centers will draw more children than the available space can accommodate. Since the learning centers will not be of equal interest, rotate groups so that all the children have an opportunity to go to popular centers. After routines have been established, children might have free choice to go where they want to, but always stress the reasons for limited numbers at each spot. If more than the specified number of participants congregate at a given center and the group seems to be enjoying the experience, forget the rules. Never permit overconcern for administration of rules and regulations to destroy the enjoyment of a learning experience.

When children are working independently on follow-up material, have an answer sheet ready for them to use in correcting their own papers. This method of self-checking accomplishes three purposes: (1) It helps them to reinforce correct answers while the work is still fresh in their minds. (2) It involves them more, since children are generally more concerned when checking their own work than they are in reviewing corrected papers from their teacher. (3) It avoids clerical depression or grading fatigue among teachers.

There are occasions when some students need additional time to finish a written assignment. Those who finish first can join the teacher in a part of the room set aside for this purpose and use this period to review a poem, play a pantomime game, or any other quiet activity. As each student finishes his work, he joins the group around the teacher. In this way you can gather your class together before beginning a new activity.

Have paper, pencils, erasers, rulers, scissors, paste, and crayons neatly arranged in places where children can help themselves. Teach them about the need to be careful when working so that materials may be used efficiently, and make them aware that if this is done the materials will be readily available when needed. Although such advice might appear simplistic, it is often overlooked when preparing children to work independently in the classroom. Since the group occupies the room for the major part of the day, it must be everybody's responsibility to keep the room neat and orderly. This, too, is a skill in which the children have to be trained and is a necessary part of group living. Before the class is dismissed, all occupants should check to see if the room is neat and the insides of their desks orderly. This exercise, a neglected part of the curriculum, will help avoid disorganization in the classroom. As Glasser (1969) has stressed, there is a need for teaching social responsibility in every school program. Responsibility and commitment are necessary where independence is the ultimate goal.

LOUD TALKING IN THE CLASSROOM

(1) Have you checked your own voice?

Do you compete with the children and outshout them? It is the least efficient means of getting their attention. There are several methods you can use. You can experiment and discover which works best for you.

Some teachers clear their throats and have trained their students to respond to this sound. Their reason for this method is that they are not always near some signal device. You can have a prearranged signal such as a bell, a chord, or series of notes on the song bells, or a quick clap of your hands. Test out the different methods and choose the one most suitable to you and to the particular group of children you have at any given time. Do not use the same method year after year. Your groups change and so should the way you do things. What might apply one year might not be applicable the next year.

When the noise level of the whole class is quite high, it is best to sit down in front of the class and speak softly. Children are very curious and will want to know what you are saying. They will hush each other unless you tell them beforehand that hushing is out of order since it creates more noise than the original one. As soon as they see your lips moving, their mouths are to close. When all the children are quiet, repeat what you were saying and bring out a card on which is written the kind of voice needed in the room at the present time (for example, "whisper" or "low voice"). You are using a quiet method that commands children's attention. This obviates the need for them to tune you out. On the contrary, they will be making an effort to try to tune you in.

(2) How high is your noise threshold?

How much is too much classroom noise? Obviously, the mere fact that you have thirty children in a room will produce a certain amount of noise. There are good noises of children being gainfully busy and active. A pilot never gets annoyed because his engine is making noises. There are bad noises that worry him and call for emergency attention (Hymes, 1955). Make sure you are not overreacting to noise that is a necessary part of the classroom environment.

(3) Have you introduced the concept of the different voice levels used for different situations?

Have the children role-play meeting a friend who is far away. What kind of voice would be used to attract his attention? What voice level would be appropriate if you were telling a friend about an outing you enjoyed? What kind if you were divulging a secret hiding place and did not want others to hear you?

Ask the students for descriptive adjectives for voices. Write their responses on sentence strips, then use them to elicit examples of situations where each adjective could be used most efficiently and the reasons for it. Make sure one of the phrases is "no voice," since there are, of course, times when no voice should be heard.

Discuss differences between space and the number of people in various situations. Ask students how many people there are in their families and how many rooms in their homes. Remind them that there are thirty or so people in the classroom and that voices competing for attention cause chaos, that each situation requires different levels of sound. Ask which voices they would use 1) in the school yard, 2) in the schoolroom during reading, 3) in the schoolroom during an art activity, 4) in the auditorium, 5) while walking home with a friend, 6) at home during a TV show or during the commercials, 7) in a dangerous situation as a warning cry.

As elementary as it sounds, many children have never investigated the reasons for suiting voice to situation. Take time to build up the rationale for the kinds of rules and regulations needed in a classroom. Remember that you do not make the laws but merely guide children in creating their rules themselves. If a child makes a law, he is automatically committing himself to upholding it. It is vitally important that you be consistent in not accepting excuses for a commitment not fulfilled (Glasser, 1969). The more time spent in this type of discussion, the less time spent in disciplinary measures.

(4) Have you used both negative and positive reinforcements?

Negative reinforcement is necessary to erase the action from the child's repertoire of reactions. If a child talks loudly while he is looking at you, frown at him and quickly shake your head. A child talking loudly to a friend should not be told to keep quiet. It is best to go over to him, touch his shoulder, and shake your head. If previous reminders do not help, move the child to another table where he can sit by himself.

There is no need to verbally reprimand the child because he already knows the meaning of your actions. The groundwork has been done during the discussions of the different types of voices and the rule of no voice. "Actions speak louder than words" is trite but true. It has often been said that children need models, not critics. The less talking you do in a disciplinary action, the more you create a disequilibrium in the child. This feeling of uneasiness has to be resolved by the child; therefore, give him a chance to think about it. The silence and your looks help him much more than recriminations.

Positive reinforcement must follow any improvement a child shows (Hunter, 1967). Many teachers use only a negative approach, but it does not create in the child the desire to follow through on any behavior modification he has made. The important phase of this behavior modification technique is to commend the child whose original undesirable behavior has been erased. When he uses a proper voice, tell him how well he is doing. For him to retain this improvement, commendation should be given regularly and often. As it becomes more and more part of his unconscious reaction, an occasional compliment will suffice.

(5) Do you use novel ideas?

To control noise levels in primary and middle grades, use a puppet as a class mascot and ask him what he thinks is wrong (McDonald and Nelson, 1955). After he whispers in your ear, ask the children to guess what he said. In this way you use the puppet to evoke comments about noise levels. Another procedure is to use a jar and lid. When it is too noisy, take the lid off without saying anything. Some child will notice and the word will be out: "The lid is off."

Tape the noise without the children being aware that the tape recorder is on. Let them hear how they sound. Elicit comments, ideas, and remedies from them as to how they can help themselves.

CONTROL OF CHILDREN WHO
CANNOT CONTROL THEMSELVES

One of the strong basic drives of the human being is that of being liked and loved. When a child lacks self-control, he knows a fuss will be made by his peers, the teacher, or both. Why should a child go against a basic drive, behaving in a way that will cause the blocking of an emotional drive he has? It is the contention here that the lack of self-control in the classroom is caused, most of the time, by the child's inability to cope with the situation in which he finds himself. Investigations into the situation should be preceded by some questions.

(1) Is there some physical reason for the disturbance?

Ask a child if he feels well. His appearance might reveal lack of sleep or the onset of illness. If you notice a lethargy in a child's movements or a defeated or dejected attitude toward you, become alerted to look for further clues that point to future trouble.

(2) Do children know what to do in a particular situation?

Are you sure your students know what is expected of them? When you give directions make sure they understand what you want. Do not simply ask, "Are there any questions?" Those children who really need clarification rarely know what to ask. Ask a few students at random to repeat the directions. If there is some confusion, then slowly go over what you have said previously. Make certain that you have included as many visual aids as possible. Spend more time at the beginning of the semester in looking for confusion when you give the directions. Some children might need smaller steps of learning. A feeling of inadequacy can cause a child to lash out and lose control of himself.

(3) Have your students helped set up the standards?

Has there been a background of understanding built to show reasons for these standards? Rules have to make sense to children. Rules are for their safety, benefit, and convenience. This is especially true of the group situation in which they find themselves. Once this has been made clear, and they accept its relevance, then they can contribute in making the laws by which they are to be governed. In making this contribution they have to make a commitment at the same time. The rules and regulations are theirs, and they are responsible for upholding them.

(4) Have you oriented the children to problem solving?

It is in the problem-solving experience that education relates to life. Ways to approach problems are vitally important learning experiences for children (Glasser, 1969). When there is a disturbance because some child lacks self-control, it helps to have his peers evaluate the situation. The teacher may act as a guide. The students can be guided into asking what went wrong. What caused the problem? What can be changed in order to bring about adherence to a particular rule? A word of caution is necessary: if intragroup hostility begins to appear, this approach should be discontinued.

Even in a congenial group, if it is one child who is to be judged by the group, there is a need for certain understandings. It is never an individual who is under attack; it is an *action* that is being investigated. Johnny does not do something without a reason. Let us try to find ways to help him avoid certain actions that might hurt him as well as others.

(5) Can you restructure the situation?

With an understanding of what to expect from children, we can structure a situation in a way that will cause as little friction as possible. Children are very egocentric; they view the world only as it relates to them and benefits them. In a class of thirty or more children, everyone wants to be first. Some children feel that they will not successfully compete, so they pull back and accept whatever they can get. If there is a spark of competitiveness in a child, then he wants to be best—always.

When children are asked to line up for dismissal, there is usually a mad dash to be first or at least second or third. There is pushing, shoving, and minor pandemonium. All teachers have heard such comments as "He got ahead of me," or "It's my turn to be first." This is true even when smaller groups are dismissed one at a time. Each child wants to be the first one in the group just dismissed. The situation can be structured by each child having his own place in line. If children are lined up according to height, they cannot argue about who got to where first. Whether a child runs or walks, he is assured of his place always being there waiting for him. A new leader can be chosen each week so that every child has the honor of being line leader at some time during the semester. Even when children are dismissed by tables, or squadrons, or how their name begins, or color of clothing, they still find their own place in line. If this structure becomes an internalized one, the children will be orderly even when the teacher is not there. A substitute might have a different way of dismissing the children. The end result will be the same because they know they have their own place in line.

This is also a good entry into the world of manners and politeness. You can introduce the magic words "Excuse me" or "Pardon me." These words automatically make people move back without a fight. People react to kindness most of the time by being kind in return. As has been wisely observed, "People are like musical instruments; the kind of music you get depends greatly on how you play."

The crux of this discussion is that when children cannot control themselves it is because they cannot cope with the situation they find themselves in. Usually they are not aware of what causes a disturbing reaction. Children are not introspective. Channeling one's frustration into socially acceptable behavior is a very sophisticated skill that most people find extremely difficult to master. How very unrealistic it would be for us to expect children to be able to do so.

If your students cannot control themselves, look for the reasons behind their loss of control. You might not be able to change their home environment, which might be a cause, but you can try to plan in advance for the kind of classroom environment that minimizes unnecessary frustrations.

REMINDING CHILDREN OF STANDARDS

Glasser (1969) believes that *involvement, relevance,* and *thinking* are the three cornerstones of education. How many teachers involve their students in building classroom standards and simultaneously make them aware of the reasons? Often the only demands made of children are that they obey the rules imposed by the teacher and considered important by the teacher.

(1) Have you investigated why rules are forgotten?

When children ignore the rules, it is usually because they are imposed without any rationale. Following rules means self-discipline—not always a pleasure-producing effort. If children do not know the need for these particular rules, why should they pay attention to them? Unless brainwashed into blind obedience, they will never show unquestioning adherence to the rules teacher thinks necessary—and that, hopefully, is not the goal educators seek. Their aim is to help develop thinkers and doers, not train obedient followers.

(2) Have you elicited standards from your students?

Take time to establish the reasons for each rule before you ask children to compose standards that should be maintained. For example, if you want them to wait for their turn to talk during discussions, then have a role-playing session in which three or four children talk out at the same time. Ask them, in their desire to be heard, what happened to their voice level? Has the audience understood what each one said? One dramatic presentation is worth a thousand teacher-words.

Build a few standards at a time. There are two reasons for this suggestion: (1) you have time to establish the rationale for each standard through role playing or discussions; and (2) smaller units of learning are absorbed more efficiently and effectively. As Hunter (1969, p. 53) states, "for efficiency in learning you work with the smallest amounts possible without sacrificing maximum meaning." Instead of making a chart with a long list of rules, write each one on a separate strip of tagboard. In this way you use each rule whenever it is needed for review.

Always couch standards in positive terms. The word "don't" is a hostile word that stresses inhibitions. While standards do inhibit some behavior, that is not their main purpose. They are primarily used to help us create a flowing environment in which the group can function most efficiently.

(3) Do you consistently review standards?

Each part of the day's program has need of definitive standards. For example, in primary grades, before children go out to recess, check the rules necessary for the playground. When they return, take two or three minutes and ask some of the children to think about their own actions in the yard. Do not ask them to tell you tales about what someone else did. Stress the fact that each child is responsible for his own actions. Explain that one can only tattle about oneself.

At the beginning of the semester take time to review every day. What you are doing, or trying to do, is establish a normative pattern of school behavior. This takes time and consistent effort at the beginning. Eventually, it is hoped, the behavior will become part of the child's system of belief and the need for review will only be an intermittent one to ensure learning.

(4) Have you evaluated, with the children's participation, how well each rule was observed?

Evaluation is a most important step in helping children internalize standards. As feedback it helps the group observe whether the rule is effective. If it is not accomplishing the result for which it was created, changes should be made. In this way children learn that when something does not work they should not just give up on it, but rather should revise, amend, or try another approach. They will be learning to solve real problems relevant to their immediate area of activity. Evaluation by the entire group makes each individual responsible for his own behavior. It is not necessary to tattle and tell tales about someone else because each person can explain at this time why he found the rule hard to adhere to. A problem-solving approach is used here rather than a judgmental one.

It is important to note here that some children might need to be excused from certain rules because of physical or emotional irregularities. The group can discuss the reasons for these dispensations. The teacher should act as a guide here and steer children away from judging. The theme is "how we can help each other."

In many instances, children learn more from each other than they do from the teacher. A case in point is when you try to help a student sing on key by humming the starting note for him. If he can't mimic, ask another student to give him the note. Most of the time, it is amazing to see how easily he can imitate his peer. Let your students help each other.

(5) Are you using positive reinforcement to help establish the rules?

It is important, especially at the time a rule is introduced, to use repetitious, positive reinforcement to help children retain what they have learned. Later only intermittent reinforcement is necessary. Although negative reinforcement might stop a child temporarily from breaking the rule, it is the positive reinforcement that makes him want to maintain the standard (Hunter, 1969).

The old saying "Nothing succeeds like success" is very true here, too. Comments on how well children are doing elicit from children tremendous effort to live up to your good opinion of them. Have you ever complimented a youngster on how nicely he is sitting or standing? Did you notice how quickly his peers tried to imitate him? If the group is complimented, they will try to repeat the performance that brought forth your commendation. Just be sure you are sincere in your commendation. Commendation should not be used as a gimmick but as feedback to children to show how well they are progressing.

(6) Are you aware of the importance of consistent review?

Never take for granted that your group will always follow the rules. Once a rule is considered learned, there is a tendency never to bring it up for discussion. If you want the classroom standards to become internalized as a system of beliefs that pertains in your classroom, you should review them from time to time. The rule has been learned, but it can be forgotten. It is up to you to refresh the children's memory. Often, after the passage of time, some standards are ready for revision. Children grow and situations change. Revising standards helps children become aware that what was needed in the past might not apply in the present. In this way the students can make a commitment to a standard knowing that it was made to suit the needs of the time, place, and people involved. They also know that nothing is static and that they have a vital share in the classroom society.

WORKING WITH CHILDREN WHO HAVE PROBLEMS

Children's problems can range in severity from temporary and slight emotional upsets, to seriously maladjusted reactions, to a world with which they cannot cope. The most important information the teacher must seek is the severity of the problem. Teachers are not child psychologists just because they deal with children and have had a smattering of college psychology courses. In most cases you are dealing with the healthy child who might need your help in guiding him to self-discovery or in helping him see a new way to approach a situation that is troubling him. If a child needs the help of a professional psychologist or psychiatrist, then it is urgent that you recognize this fact without trying to speak authoritatively in a field outside your ken.

(1) Are you child-oriented?

This question might seem ridiculous, but experience has shown that many teachers do not spend enough time in watching children and listening to them. A few years ago, a group of teachers was attending a demonstration of a class in session. They were instructed to focus on any child who caught their attention and were to report on that child's activities during a thirty-minute period. When they were asked for the reports, it was found that the majority of teachers had been focusing their attention on things rather than on children: they had busily copied down bulletin-board ideas, teacher-made games, and teaching techniques. Teachers may get so involved in the "how-to" that they lose sight of the importance of the individual child.

Look, listen, and record! In a sense, it is easy for you to watch the child because he may be involved in an activity and therefore unaware that he is being observed. He is in his everyday world and not in a totally new environment. Here is the time to jot down his reaction to a peer or how he approaches and gets involved in an activity. The teacher can get significant clues that could help him in his diagnosis.

A child is considered maladjusted when he feels so frustrated in need of satisfaction that he cannot function intellectually in an effective manner and he cannot meet the social conventions and demands of his environment (Blackham, 1968). He reveals his anxiety by his lack of ability to concentrate and by his tense behavior. A very obvious clue is his hyperactivity, which far surpasses the normal activeness of children. Any extreme actions, overreaction to minor incidents, or rigid and withdrawn behavior should be noted. Does he show an extreme need for your constant approval? Does he refuse to do any schoolwork or expose himself in any competitive field? These symptoms cry out "Notice me, I'm having trouble!"

Record moments of stress and the incident that seemed to cause it. Jot down any unusual comment the child has made. Is there a difference in his behavior during informal times, such as recess, music, or art? In which area does he reveal his problem? Is it in the academic area or in the social area that he seems to have most of his difficulties? Record incidents and dates and do not use vague descriptions. If you write that he is listless, describe the actions that prompted you to give that opinion. What might seem extreme to you might be viewed as normal by someone else; therefore be descriptive in your records.

It is not hard to keep anecdotal records. The trick is to have a small pad and pencil within hand's reach. It takes a second to jot down a reminder, which can be elaborated on in more detail at a later time. A few minutes every day can be devoted to transferring the information onto an index card that you have for every child in your class. After a month or so a quick check through the cards will reveal which children require special attention. This check is an important feedback for the teacher. A small incident added to what has happened previously can be of value in ferreting out a possible cause revealed by asocial or atypical behavior.

(2) Do you diagnose the problem?

Check whether the child has any physical or intellectual deficiencies. At the beginning of the year watch for signs of poor sight or poor hearing. One obvious clue is squinting. Does the child hold printed materials too close or too far away from his eyes? Does he hold the book off to one side? Stand behind him and softly whisper his name. Watch for heads turned to one side when children are listening to a story. This can reveal a hearing problem. Many children who show difficulties in learning in the primary grades will also reveal difficulties in their perceptual motor development. To discover this weakness, put a few strips of masking tape on the floor to simulate a walking board and ask each child to walk forward, one foot in front of another, and then walk backward the same way. Ask the child to skip, hop, and jump while you look for abnormalities (Kephart, 1960). Does he seem to be unusually tired? A simple way to ascertain whether he is getting enough sleep is to ask about the television programs he watches. Is he hungry? Informal discussions about what we eat for breakfast and when we go to sleep can give you information in this area.

If a child has a history of poor academic performance, listen to his comments during free and relaxed discussion periods. Are his ideas disconnected? Is his judgment appropriate for his age? It is during discussion periods that the teacher can notice discrepancies between academic attainment and reasoning abilities.

Investigate whether the child's problem is of long duration. Make a note of what previous teachers have done to help him. Have they found one approach more helpful than others? Try not to repeat the failures of the previous year.

Invite parents to a conference. If they refuse to come, this act might be a clue. Their refusal might indicate a lack of confidence in the teacher's ability to help their child. It could be evidence of parental feelings of inadequacy. A teacher might need the help of the resource people that the principal might recommend. When they do come, let them do most of the talking. A positive way to start the discussion is to mention an area in which the child is successful. Ask for the child's reaction to school. What does he talk about at home? What are his special interests? What do the parents enjoy about the child? What hopes do they have for him? What upsets the child? How do they handle him when he is upset? Listen—and later record what they said, or your impressions of what they said, being sure to label them your impressions. Do not infuse any of your personal value system. It is the parents' value system that is most important because of the influence it has on their child.

The watching and listening might help you find a way to alleviate a problem situation. But even if it does not, it will help you become an efficient observer, and the product of your observations will aid others in serving the child. Above and beyond all else, you will be paying more attention to children.

(3) Are you aware of the professional help available to you?

Request a meeting with your principal, nurse, and school counselor. Each member of the team can contribute additional information that might help you find a solution to problems a student is having.

Come to the meeting with objective, anecdotal records in which you have written the actions and reactions of the child. This is no place for opinions and charges. If these records show an objective reporting of incidents, the experts might be able to add them to their files as source material from which to diagnose and plan ways to help the child.

The nurse usually checks on the child's medical history; the counselor reviews information on his academic ability. Both may make contact with the parents or make home visits, and thus gather additional insights.

It is at these meetings that decisions can be made as to whether medical help is needed. There are agencies that operate guidance clinics to which the parent can be referred and where a child can be assisted by trained professionals.

For the child who has a severe problem, your main role is to identify him so that he can receive the proper professional help.

LACK OF RESPECT FOR AUTHORITY

(1) Have you investigated possible reasons for this lack of respect?

Is it triggered during interactions with all adults in his environment? He might be angry with his parents and therefore lashes out at them through other parent figures. In this case, the adult is not the cause but the target of his anger. It is also possible that respectful attitudes have not been transmitted to him either by precept or by models in his home environment. Therefore, these attitudes have not been built into his behavior patterns. If his disrespectful attitude is shown toward you only, you must look for some action on your part. Have you let him down at the time when he needed support? Have you inadvertently been unfair to him and not given him a chance to explain? He might have felt diminished and reacted that way to protect himself. Remember the saying, "The best defense is a good offense."

A child who feels backed into a corner will fight back. When he feels he cannot cope with the anger and hostility directed at him and cannot find a way to retreat, he will attack verbally, and even physically, in extreme cases. This behavior is not true of all children, but is of those labeled "disrespectful."

(2) Has respect been earned?

The first step in training children to be respectful is by being an example of good manners. If you want them to listen without interrupting, it behooves you to do the same when they are speaking. Respect a child's uniqueness and give him authority in certain areas and abide by his decisions. The area of his jurisdiction must be circumscribed so that there will be a chance for his ideas to be followed. For example, ask the supplies monitor to give his opinion of the best way to pass out materials. Help him with his thinking and when he has decided (with your guidance) on the best way, announce that Johnny will tell the class how to obtain supplies because he is in charge of that department. One word of caution: Delegating authority can only be done after children have learned not to abuse the privilege. If a child oversteps his authority he loses his position. Do not assume that all children are aware of this rule. Teach it as a necessary skill for successful group living.

Besides needing models, students need training in developing coping behavior. Frustration, anger, resentment, unfairness will be part of their life experiences. Help them learn to handle themselves during these trying times.

(3) Have you tried the following approaches?

Demonstrations through role playing show children patterns of behavior that might not be in their reaction repertoire. Children might not have been exposed to ideas of respect for others, or even to the concept of self-respect. During a class meeting discuss how one might react to some unintended unfairness on the part of a person in authority. What would you do if you were blamed for something you did not do? Children do have individual ways in which they handle their emotions. Let them hear and learn from each other.

Teach them that what a person sees depends on where he is standing. A good place to dramatize this concept is on the playground in the four-square area. One of the rules is that the ball must not touch the line when it is bounced into the next box. From some places of the square it would seem that the ball did touch the line. In another place the ball is seen as hitting the ground a few inches away from the line. Things are not always what they seem to be. When seen in this perspective, a cry of unfairness is not always deserved.

Planned ignoring is a technique that helps in some situations (Smith and Hudgins, 1964). A sudden outburst that seems almost involuntary and surprises the child, too, should be ignored. Unless it acts as a contagious incitement that will spread throughout the classroom, it is best to make believe the outburst was not heard. Feigned deafness on the part of the teacher is a most efficient reaction when a student is deliberately trying to provoke hostility from him.

Try to avoid the kind of confrontation that ends in the child defiantly saying, "I won't do it!" If this conflict happens, state that you do not believe in force. Walk away from him and use a diversionary action that will interest your group, thus taking away the child's audience. Get a quiet game started and when the children are involved, try to welcome the child back. Explain that he is part of the group and is needed. If he does not respond, he might need more time to cool off. Invite him to go to the library table, to get busy with another activity, or even to stay where he is, but do not wait for his reaction. Go back to the group and get everyone involved in an activity.

Avoid threats. In some cases you cannot carry them out since you are not the school's policy maker. Even if you were, most children react with a "so what" or "big deal" attitude. In the long run, threats are not effective behavior deterrents.

Be wary of the "big shot" initiator. He takes pleasure in starting irritating noises such as foot-tapping, chair-scraping, funny mouth noises. These noises can spread like wildfire and mere requests for quiet can easily be ignored because most of the time you are not quite sure who is making the noises since they are being done surreptitiously. Stop all activity and discuss the part distracting noises play in wasting time. Or entice students by telling them of a popular activity they will soon be able to participate in if the noises stop. Make sure the activity is one they usually beg to do, and be sure to follow through on your promises. Some people might call this act giving into bribery, but there is an underlying principle involved: there is a time for work and a time for play, and fooling around during working time makes students forfeit playtime.

In his multifaceted role, it is hard for the teacher to skillfully balance all the goals he wants to attain. He often finds that behavioral problems block his attempt to reach instructional objectives. Unless these problems are solved, little learning will occur in the classroom.

THE ANGRY AND BELLIGERENT CHILD

Children are not born angry. There are irritants and frustrations within their environment that are possible causes for this reaction. Teachers have to approach these angry children with several basic understandings.

First, the teacher must consider his own reactions to the child's anger and hostility. Can he understand that he is not the target? Can he assume the role of a therapist and sense, as well as seek, what the child is really asking for?

Second, children come from varied backgrounds. They will use the same tricks on you to elicit the kind of behavior they get from their parents. Will you fall into their trap or will you step back a few paces and react with objective deliberation?

Third, you will not always have time to use preventative methods or forestall certain actions, but you must be aware of the different approaches that can help the child and be on the lookout for the signals that children send out.

Fourth, you are helped in your investigation in that you see the child in both casual and intensive activities. Teachers often become part of the surroundings and children are not aware of their presence. During these times children are not putting on shows and reveal themselves to you if you are a skillful observer.

Finally, you are not going to solve all problems. But you will be able to help some children, and this fact will sustain you in your failures.

(1) Is the irritant a physical problem?

Children have different frustration levels. Some can tolerate more than others, but a tired child's frustration tolerance plummets. He is crankier than normal and less able to cope with the upsets that are likely to occur in interpersonal relations or in learning activities. If a child has not had enough sleep, do not make too many demands on him. Provide a relaxed program for him. Informal anecdotes elicited from children on how they feel when they are tired may lead to the importance of rest and how much sleep one should get for optimum health or vitality.

Children, especially in the primary grades, might not be able to express the fact they do not feel well. They will show it in their abnormal reactions. Look into the child's eyes. Are they red or glazed? Does he look flushed and feel warm to your touch?

(2) Is this behavior a cry for attention?

Some children become belligerent in order to be noticed because they feel deprived of attention. Investigate a student's perception of his family relationships. Many times children misread or misjudge an action and think they are unloved. If the behavior is new, it might be due to a crisis at home. Perhaps his home life is hectic now and he is being ignored because of a divorce or a new baby. Investigate his peer relationships, because they might be going through a change. His best friend might have found a new buddy and shifted his loyalties accordingly. If one of the above is true, try making him important by a little extra attention such as verbal appreciation of some of his qualities. Ask for his help in jobs that children enjoy doing with the teacher. One word of caution: Be subtle with your attentions. Do not let him be called "teacher's pet."

(3) Does the child feel adequate?

Children subjected to standards beyond their physical, mental, and emotional maturity can be so frustrated in their efforts to please that they develop tremendous feelings of aggression. Did anything happen in school to make a child feel stupid? Does he experience success in at least one area—such as in passing out books, papers, and so on, or in erasing or writing words on the chalk board? If a child answers a question incorrectly, do you take time to lead him to the proper answer, or do you immediately call on someone to correct him? Children's egos are sensitive and vulnerable. Help them build and maintain their self-esteem. Judicious questions can help in eliciting information that will help children be proud of their contribution. Then again, the acts of probing, searching, and thinking are more important than instant answers, whether given by the teacher or by the child's peers.

Is the angry child being victimized by a bully with whom he cannot cope? Perhaps his outbursts are provoked by the child sitting near him. Be aware that a "Mr. Innocence" can be a hidden pincher and an undercover troublemaker. Change seats and see if the outbursts subside.

Construct a sociogram to see how well his peers like him as well as to determine his preferences. The child who is an isolate may be lost in the group and you might not be aware of his low status. If you know that he is unpopular, you might be able, through indirect means, to elevate him to a better standing among his classmates. Requesting the social reject to help you choose a game or a child to start a game are indirect ways of conferring status. Children begin to seek the reasons for teacher's preference and thus become aware of qualities they did not see at first. Some children think no one likes them; a sociogram can reveal how true or false such impressions are. Be aware that it is a child's feelings about his lack of self-worth that set off negative reactions. The sociogram is

another evaluative instrument, one that may help you uncover a cause for an
aggressive action or a possible reason for withdrawn behavior.

(4) What kind of emotional tone do you set in your classroom?

Have you created an environment of acceptance and understanding? Have you
shown that you enjoy your students and can relax with them? Have you tried to
inculcate in your students the philosophy that asks "How can we help each
other?"

Do you try to talk to each child often enough? It is a good idea to have a
check list on which you can record some personal contacts you have had each
day. It might surprise you to find that there are some children to whom you pay
very little attention. By your actions to help and understand your students, you
will provide them with a model and motivate them to help and understand each
other. Children will accept demands and will try to fulfill their responsibilities
in group living if they like you and feel you like them.

(5) Can the child help in diagnosing the problem?

Listen to his complaints and try to determine what is bothering him. Be
available for private talks with him. Ask him to help you in chores you do after
the rest of the class is dismissed. During this time, certain casual questions
might be of help in starting the discussion. What does he enjoy most at school?
What are some of the things or situations he finds most annoying? Bring in a
story of what you did not like when you were a student. A relaxed and
open-ended discussion might help him express his frustrations.

Use sentence completion forms that trigger emotional reactions: "I get angry
when . . ." "I hate to . . ." "I wish I could . . ." "When I look into the mirror
I . . ." The answers might give you additional clues to what causes the anger
that explodes into belligerent or aggressive behavior.

Whom does the youngster admire? Who are his heroes? He might be
patterning his behavior after a "tough guy" adult who is pugnacious and
belligerent. Use an open discussion on favorite heroes and lead the children into
the topic of qualities that make a true leader. Do not lecture; lead the
discussions so that children do most of the talking.

Remove a child from a situation that causes him to become overexcited. Any
area in your room that is set aside can be used as a temporary isolation area: a
library corner or a table away from other children. Explain that the removal is
not a punishment but a chance to calm down and relax. A quiet atmosphere
may help him gain control. Removing him will also prevent a contagious effect
on the other children.

Punishing the aggressive child breaks down his controls even more and
increases the existing resentment. Be sparing of punishment and lavish with

understanding. When he voices his complaints, repeat what he says. You are not agreeing with him. What you are doing is listening and reacting to what he says. In many cases, this response acts like a soothing balm on injured feelings and calms the child. If you do get angry, let the child know it is the action you dislike, not him. Never attack him verbally (Ginott, 1965).

You must be aware of the intensity of the child's problem. If it is too deep for him to handle alone, you should ask for help from the school counselor as soon as possible. If a child's action consistently triggers a highly emotional response from you, it would be advisable to ask for a transfer of the child to another class. When this is not possible, consider that you might be part of the problem. Perhaps it might help you to discipline yourself.

Sensitivity to the individuality of students helps the teacher develop an alertness to the signals that trigger belligerent behavior. Preventative measures usually reduce aggressive reactions.

THE WITHDRAWN CHILD

The "hard to reach" child, with whom it is difficult to establish a two-way communication, is the student who observes rather than participates. Apathy and lack of interest are symptoms of his withdrawal. He is usually shy, timid, and conforming. Because of these characteristics he can often go unnoticed, yet it is important that he be noticed. Such behavior can be true of most children in certain situations and at particular times in their development. However, if it becomes pronounced, it may indicate that the child needs more help than the teacher can give.

(1) What are possible causes for withdrawn behavior?

Often these children are "emotional dropouts," hiding behind a wall of defenses they have built because of feelings of inadequacy. They have dropped out because of the extreme anxieties they feel trying to live up to the ambitions others imposed on them. Children will withdraw from demands or situations that they believe they cannot cope with successfully. If they have experienced many failures, their feelings of inadequacy are heightened and their self-esteem is lowered.

Another reason a child may withdraw is that the adults in his environment may be too rigid in their demand for obedience. These demands may cause him to place strong controls on his impulses which allow for no flexibility in his behavior. He lives with a constant fear of inability to control spontaneous impulse and therefore suppresses free interaction. Since emotional satisfactions are not available in his relationship with others, he will sometimes turn to the world of fantasy, where he can be king. Such children are the daydreamers; they have tuned the world out.

(2) Have you made the child feel secure and comfortable?

The quality of the teacher-child relationship is of utmost importance. It must be a consistent one without emotional extremes and one that the child can count on. Be aware that it takes time to build a rapport with a child. You should move slowly and not overwhelm the child emotionally.

(3) Are you reinforcing the behavior that will help the child?

The withdrawn student does not disrupt the group. On the contrary, he hides behind a colorless façade. Avoid holding him up as a model of good behavior. This reinforces his shyness. Concentrate praise on the times he might venture forth orally to ask a question, or possibly make a comment. Watch for overt reactions no matter how tentative and see if by some means you can help him express himself. Again, this must be in a relaxed and casual way.

(4) Have you capitalized on his successful accomplishment?

If at all possible, ask him to help another child or small group of children who might be experiencing difficulties in an area in which he excels. You are helping to build his self-esteem by placing a value on his contributions to others as well as making him aware of his own strengths.

(5) Are your expressed thoughts clear, concise, and explicit?

When you are giving directions or explaining a concept, be very clear. Explain each step in detail, using concrete materials whenever possible. A withdrawn child's shyness might prevent him from asking questions to clarify a misunderstanding. This leads to mistakes and future failures, which reinforce his feelings of inadequacy.

(6) Do you guide the withdrawn child to interact with children who are compatible with him?

In helping the student relate to his peers, try to pair him with children who are somewhat like him in personality. An aggressive and domineering peer will overwhelm him and he will withdraw into the very reaction you are trying to help him overcome. As he gains confidence within a small group, you can try to widen and broaden the group within which he can optimally function.

(7) Do you expose him to a variety of media with which he can express himself?

If he has difficulty in expressing himself orally, let him express himself in art. Use some success-guaranteed approaches. For example, ask him to fold a white or buff-colored manila paper in half. After he opens the paper tell him to dribble a few dots of colored tempera on it. Three different colors make the results very attractive. Ask him to close the paper and gently rub the top cover. The results look like Rorschach blots and there are no failures. Everyone has interesting results to show regardless of their ability in art.

This exercise can also be used as a creative writing assignment. Ask the child what the picture looks like to him and have him write about it. While teachers are not trained to interpret reactions to blots, a child's answer might reveal creative, witty, or even bizarre answers compared to those of the rest of the class.

Another fail-proof art technique is the "scribble picture." The student scribbles on a paper and then colors in the spaces with different colors. When these scribbles are cut out and mounted on another paper, they look very attractive and give the effect of abstract art. Here too there are no failures. These successes are very important in helping heal a bruised ego.

(8) Are you availing yourself of the help parents can give?

Try to establish a good working relationship with the parents so that you can try to help them understand the child's behavior. They might not be aware of different positive approaches they could use. The parents can also give you a clue to how much the genes or home environment are operating here. Is the parent an introvert, a shy, uncommunicative person? If you are a good listener you can learn a great deal during meetings with parents. When school and home work hand in hand, results can be obtained sooner and more easily.

It is of vital import that you assess the severity of the child's maladjustment so that you do not try to stem an avalanche of problems with crude tools and inadequate knowledge.

CASE INCIDENTS

Case incident 1: The attention demander

Joe was a member of an extremely well-behaved sixth-grade class, an above-average student, and an active participant in the classroom.

Although Joe performed well in class, he demanded a great deal of personal attention. When he obtained this attention, his behavior was satisfactory. However, when left to work on his own without personal encouragement by the teacher, he constantly disturbed the class. For example, he would yell "Wait!" in the middle of a spelling class or interrupt the teacher while she was giving a lesson.

He was reprimanded for the following behavior: kicking his classmates during reading, pushing them while they were standing in line, and fighting with other boys on the playground. One day the teacher on playground duty asked him to stop misbehaving. His reply: "You can't tell me what to do. You're not my teacher!"

His teacher threatened to send a note home to his mother, but Joe appeared unconcerned. Not able to tolerate his behavior any longer, the teacher called his mother to school for a conference. During the meeting, his mother stated: "Joe's father and I do not feel that a child should be inhibited; therefore, we allow him to express his feelings openly and freely. We spend a great deal of time with him and consider ourselves to be a close-knit family unit. We feel freedom will enable him to become a better adjusted individual."

Discussion Questions. Do Joe's two worlds of home and school conflict? How? Should a teacher criticize a parent's philosophy of child rearing? If so, how should he approach the parent? How would you approach a child in the above situation?

STUDENT NOTES

Case incident 2: The noise makers

The morning bell had just sounded and Mrs. Nolan's class was entering the room. Noisily the children took their seats.

"Tommy," Mrs. Nolan said, "will you please lead us in the flag salute?"

There was continued noise and shuffling of chairs as Tommy came to the front of the room. After standing for a few minutes, the children finally quieted down and the flag salute was given. More noise was heard as the children took their seats and continued to talk.

Mrs. Nolan came to the front of the room to present the morning assignment and immediately began in a loud voice, attempting to talk over the still noisy students. After part of the directions were given, the class became quieter. When Mrs. Nolan finished the directions, she asked, "Now, are there any questions about what you are to do?" Immediately a number of hands began waving madly, and Mrs. Nolan proceeded to repeat the entire set of directions. Finally the class began to work.

At the end of the thirty minutes she had allotted for the math lesson, Mrs. Nolan observed that few students were near completion. Frustrated, she nevertheless told the children, "Put away your math papers and please take out your reading books. Those people in Group 1 remain at your seats and read silently, Group 2 please pick partners and read to each other, and Group 3 come to the back table for your reading check."

All the while she was giving instructions, desk tops were being slammed and books opened and closed.

A voice shouted, "Where does Group 2 go?"

Another voice—"I didn't hear what I'm supposed to do."

Loudly, Mrs. Nolan asked for the class's attention and repeated the instructions. Again, the children began working until the first recess bell rang.

As the children returned from recess, the noise began again. Balls were thrown in the ball cupboard. Janet dropped her sweater, and Brian stepped on it as he tried to beat Gregory to his seat. The clamor continued as Mrs. Nolan took her position at the front of the room and began giving instructions to continue their reading, everyone at his own seat. She then returned to her desk to finish correcting the autobiographies the children had turned in the day before. However, a great deal of fidgeting was going on, students asked to go to the rest room, and a line formed at the drinking fountain.

"Will everyone please take his seat," Mrs. Nolan pleaded. "If you have finished your reading assignment, please take out your library book and read quietly."

The room was relatively quiet, but a low buzz could be heard. "I've finished my library book," one student announced. "What do I do now, Mrs. Nolan?"

As she sensed the restlessness, Mrs. Nolan tried to remedy the situation by proceeding to the next subject. "Will everyone please put away his reading book, and, Nancy, will you please pass out the paper for the spelling test." As Nancy passed out the paper, the students began chattering. When the paper was finally all passed out, Mrs. Nolan began the test.

The pattern continued throughout the remainder of the day—with Mrs. Nolan becoming more and more tense and frustrated as she continually asked for quiet. It seemed that whenever the class activity was to change from one subject to the next, there were a few minutes of unnecessary noise and confusion, and often directions had to be repeated before the children could begin working. The day seemed rushed and no assignment was easily completed within the allotted time period.

Discussion Questions. Can you suggest better methods of presenting assignments and obtaining attention? Why were none of the assignments completed? Suggest some good types of activities to be used after recess to settle a class down.

STUDENT NOTES

Case incident 3: How much to give and what to take

An emotionally handicapped student poses special problems for many teachers. He requires special attention and consideration. In many cases, the teacher may not know any reason for the child's emotional disturbances and therefore any action taken must be done cautiously.

Consider a fourth grader named Paul. A student in Mrs. Johnson's class, Paul had to see a special teacher for the emotionally handicapped every day. At times he could perform any assignment quickly with high aptitude, and would then seem like a very normal, healthy boy with no problems at all. However, at other times he would throw tantrums and be very difficult to deal with.

Often he absolutely refused to do an assignment. After thoroughly explaining a lesson to the whole class and passing out dittos with exercises on them, Mrs. Johnson would notice that everyone was working except Paul. When asked why he wasn't writing the answers, he would simply reply, "I don't want to" and put his head down on the desk. This kind of attitude often disrupted the entire class. When Mrs. Johnson didn't force him to work, the others asked why they had to work. Paul was usually a "loner" but occasionally associated with Henry, a boy who attended the emotionally handicapped classes with him. Sometimes the two boys refused to do anything or to talk to anybody.

Mrs. Johnson was able to learn a little about Paul's home life and discovered that he had two mentally retarded brothers. His mother often left home and was not seen for days. Both of his parents frequently threatened the boy and constantly punished him. One day Paul came back into the classroom at 3:20. All students were to have reported home by 3:10 and were to stay off school grounds. Paul said he had just walked around without going home. He wanted Mrs. Johnson to write a note for him to his mother saying he had been at school with the teacher for the twenty minutes he was late. He was afraid his mother would hit him for not coming home.

Many times Paul would start shaking in the middle of class or get into a violent mood while playing one of the games at recess.

Discussion Questions. How can Mrs. Johnson handle this situation? She must give Paul special attention without involving the rest of the class. She cannot allow his actions to disturb a whole morning of work, yet punishing him might bring hostile reactions. She knows that providing him with an excuse for his parents is interfering, but is afraid of the consequences if she does not. She knows that Paul has the ability to be a fairly good student, but that he is hindered by these emotional disturbances. Should she cater to him when he gets in one of his moods? Ignore them? Punish him?

STUDENT NOTES

Case incident 4: Belligerent Bill

Bill consistently seemed to be fighting with his fifth-grade classmates, and Mrs. Harris, his teacher, was always correcting him for this behavior. He was also very impatient. When he answered correctly, and the teacher acknowledged this fact, he repeated the answer several times so that his classmates were able to hear. He had a very domineering personality and enjoyed showing off his abilities. For example, before another child had time to respond to a question, Bill would blurt out the answer. He often made comments such as, "This book is *so* simple.

How come he's so stupid? Why can't he answer? It's so *easy*." He did this so emphatically that he implied to the others that they were not nearly as intelligent as he.

Bill was easily upset over the smallest incidents. On one occasion he asked John, "Where's your eraser?" When John did not answer, Bill began to shove him. After the two struggled for awhile, Bill complained to Mrs. Harris: "John's stingy. He won't let me use his eraser." Mrs. Harris replied, "Bill, are you fighting again? You can't seem to get along with anyone, can you?"

On another occasion Bill was asked to collect a set of papers from each person in the class. Karen had not completed the assignment and told Bill, "Come back later. I'm not finished." Bill became indignant and said, "Teacher told me to collect them. Give it to me *now*." Bill reached for it and after a struggle, the assignment was torn. Bill then told Mrs. Harris, "Karen tore her paper—not my fault. She wouldn't give me her paper." Mrs. Harris said, "Bill, you're fighting again. You even fight with girls. Now, apologize to Karen. Tell her you are sorry and that you'll come back for her paper when you have finished collecting the others."

Bill initiated many arguments with his classmates. He was constantly being corrected and punished for his aggressive behavior, yet scolding had no effect on him.

Discussion Questions. What are the possible reasons for his behavior? Can you suggest a possible plan of action that might modify his behavior? List some causes of aggressive behavior.

STUDENT NOTES

Case incident 5: Where do I belong?

Marcos was a third-grade student working below grade level. No records had been found to show that he had had any schooling. It may have been that his real family were migrant workers and he was never at any one school long enough to accumulate a record, or it was possible he had never been to school at all.

As for Marcos's level of performance, his math and spelling were at first-grade level, he showed no reading ability, both his cursive and printed writing were slow and painfully done, and he showed no interest of any kind in English or social studies.

Other children in the class teased Marcos about his being behind and having to do the "easy math." Marcos tried to compensate by attempting to make himself look and feel superior, answering, for instance, by saying he could do better than they in other subject areas. He also tried to prove himself outside the classroom during recess. He picked fights with younger boys, disrupted other students' games, and even tried to hold the bathroom door shut so he had power over who got in and out. Such actions resulted in his being labeled a "real discipline problem" by many teachers.

The fact that Marcos was so far behind, and that no learning desire whatsoever could be inspired, made Marcos a candidate for individual testing. The results showed that no mental handicap was present, and that the major problem was related to his limited educational background.

Marcos's class was large, so that individual attention by the teacher was difficult. However, a visiting student teacher, working individually with Marcos, was able to increase his performance level in writing and math. She always made their work together intensive, consistently making Marcos direct all of his attention toward what they were doing, almost constantly pushing him so that his mind would not wander.

The challenge and immediate reinforcement were perhaps what Marcos needed to make him work. Unfortunately, there was no special type of classroom at the school for pupils such as Marcos who needed special individual attention.

Discussion Questions. Help for Marcos must come now while he is still young. But what is his problem? Would you recommend additional testing? What kind? Should Marcos be retained in the third grade? What factors should be considered in deciding whether to retain a student? Can retention affect the social development of a student? Can the "labeling" effects of retention be reduced? To what extent should parents and the child be included in decisions regarding retention? What research is available concerning the retention of students? Does retention help or hinder students?

Case incident 6: The student teacher blues

Mr. Young, a student teacher, took over a class for the first time. The students were told in clear-cut terms by the regular teacher to give Mr. Young their complete cooperation. Needless to say, several of the students were not threatened by the prospect of Mr. Young's making a report on them to their regular teacher.

Ronnie, the terror of the class and a painful thorn in the side of any teacher, was the principal instigator of all the trouble. Ronnie chose that morning to be more active and wilder than usual. In less than two hours, Ronnie socked Mark in the stomach, punched Debra in the throat, and spat water all over Frank's shirt. He just would not sit down.

Some of the other students began to follow suit. They saw Ronnie deliberately doing all these things to disrupt the class and getting away with it, so they, too, joined the bandwagon. All Mr. Young's attempts to discourage Ronnie from any more rough antics failed; and he was consequently gradually losing control of the class. Having the children put their heads down on their desks did not do much good. Nor did writing down the names of the troublemakers and giving them "unhappy faces" next to their names. Nor raising his voice without yelling to show them his disapproval.

When the regular teacher returned, Mr. Young asked him what an "inexperienced" teacher's aide could do when a child said "Make me!" If the number one rule of discipline was to be consistent and follow through—to mean what one said and not make empty threats—what could Mr. Young have done, outside of physical force, to make Ronnie sit down long enough to leave his classmates alone? Physical force, Mr. Young believed, was not really the answer to anything, but Ronnie had actually dared him to make him stop it and sit down. "Being merely a student teacher," Mr. Young said, "I did not and still do not know what my 'rights' are. Can a teacher use physical force to discipline a problem child? Should he really use force, though? Are there other alternatives?"

Discussion Questions. What are the conditions that arise for an "inexperienced" teacher to lose control of a class? What should a teacher do when it happens? How does he regain control? How does he keep from losing control again? How would you answer Mr. Young's question?

STUDENT NOTES

Case incident 7: Decisions for diagnosis

It was the first period of the day for a fifth-grade class, and about twenty-five children were present. After the shuffle of finding seats had subsided, the teacher instructed the students to open their books to a story for an oral reading lesson. Going systematically around the room, she called on the students to read aloud. Their performance level ranged from proficiency to uncertainty, but most of the children read smoothly and with understanding.

But soon it was Mary's turn. The teacher asked her to read just a couple of sentences, but it took her as long to say them as for most children to read a paragraph. Mary was an awkward stutterer. She fidgeted and seemed to be undergoing a great emotional strain while reading. It was difficult for an observer to overlook the stuttering and her discomfort to take notice of what she was reading, but it became evident that Mary had a perception problem as well. In just those two or three sentences, she misread two words that were central to the story; she read "untied" as "united" and "inch" as "chin." Mary's teacher corrected her mistakes, thanked her for reading, and asked Martin to conclude the paragraph.

That afternoon the class worked on a written exercise. Later, while grading the papers, the teacher observed that Mary had transcribed "there" as "three" and consistently switched the medial letters around to produce a completely different word than the one she saw on the printed page.

The combination of this perceptual problem and the stuttering placed Mary under an enormous handicap.

Discussion Questions. Does Mary have an emotional or physical problem? How can this problem be diagnosed? What are some causes of stuttering? of perceptual problems? What developmental information should be obtained? Can such problems be solved in a normal classroom? Should such a student be recommended for a special class? What factors should be considered in making the decision? Who should be involved in it?

STUDENT NOTES

Case incident 8: A teller of tales

Richard, a large child for his age, was the most compulsive tattler in his kindergarten class. He was the source of constant class disruption, since his minor outbursts occurred at unpredictable times and would not cease until acknowledged. He was completely preoccupied, during both class and recess, with reporting the small inconsistencies of his peers. His constant pleas for

"Teacher! Teacher!" expressed alarm, though they usually related to insignificant offenses. The teacher tried to handle the problem by ignoring him or responding negatively with "Richard, please don't worry about the other children, just worry about yourself." Such tactics slightly decreased Richard's tattling behavior, but it was still a major problem in the class and he was quickly losing favor with the other children.

The teacher was aware that at home Richard was the eldest of four children, and his mother, often preoccupied with household duties, had instructed him to report all rule infractions by his younger siblings. He was never allowed to discipline the children by himself—only to supervise them and to inform his mother of any activity falling outside the strict limits he imposed. It was difficult for Richard to differentiate between his responsibilities at home and at school. His supervising duties at home interfered with his social relations in school.

Discussion Questions.   How can the teacher convince Richard of the differing responsibilities associated with differing environments? How could she clarify the insignificance of the tattled occurrences to him? How could she convince him of the equality of his peers, and of their mutual capacity for responsibility and self-control? Do some elementary school teachers reinforce tattling? How? What are some appropriate plans to counteract this problem?

STUDENT NOTES

Chapter Three

EFFECTIVE USE OF TIME AND SELF

Often a teacher's first teaching position is also his first contact in working for a large organization, with all the attendant record keeping and other activities purported to be essential to keeping it running. You may encounter some problems in this area whose solutions depend less on diagnosis; hence, in this chapter, you will find less emphasis on diagnostic questions. Instead, we will give greater attention to some plans and routines that might help you reconcile your individual life-style to institutional requirements.

TIME FOR PLANNING AND PREPARATION

Any new endeavor needs a plan of operation—and this is especially true for the teacher. The beginning of each year is a new event for all teachers, regardless of number of years' experience, because every new class has different students with different problems requiring diagnosis and prescriptive teaching. This diagnostic-prescriptive approach requires much planning and preparation. You will find it helpful to organize the initial operations of your program so as to be free to accomplish the above.

(1) Have you made a realistic appraisal of your work load for the coming year?

Teachers are required to spend a set number of hours in school, but their working hours, of course, include a great deal of extra time outside of school. Know before you start that your work will require more time than you thought it would. If you are studying for an advanced degree, do not take more units than you can handle. At the beginning of the semester, you may be refreshed by a vacation and feel up to handling your work and a busy school schedule too. Be aware, however, that the stored-up energy will dwindle because the first month of school can be an exhausting time. There are unexpected overloads of work, both in courses taken at school and in duties in your teaching job. Be realistic in making demands on yourself. Do not become frustrated and thus shortchange your students by trying to do too much at one time.

(2) Have you taken time to plan for the new semester?

During the summer develop ideas and materials for interest centers (see Chap. 4), bulletin boards, and independent activities. Prepare games and manipulative activities that involve children so that you will be free to observe them while they are working. In addition, be sure to obtain the records of your new students the week before school starts.

Make a master sheet of the names of your students and run off several copies. These lists will be useful in many ways—as attendance sheets at the beginning of the year; as check lists to see that you have included all the children in groupings, room duties, and committee work; and as check lists for the return of homework assignments.

Use the week before school to organize yourself and prepare your room. This will free you from involvement with miscellanea the first week and give you time to observe and interact with your students. Some suggested ways to prepare yourself are as follows.

(a) Look through cumulative records for the reading levels of your new students. This information will be helpful in selecting reading material.

(b) Check which social studies units have been studied and plan guidelines for discussing the concepts that were learned. This information will help you determine how much review is needed.

(c) Obtain expendable supplies and books. Become familiar with the audiovisual equipment available. Look into schedules for the use of film and filmstrip projectors.

(d) Plan your room layout. Set up an attractive library corner. If possible, have a listening center ready for use on the first day of school, as well as interest areas for science, math, language arts, and art work (see Chap. 4). Have expendable supplies such as papers, pencils, erasers, crayons, and scissors placed where they are easily accessible.

(e) Put up your bulletin boards. Keep them simple because after the first week there will be student work available to display.

Plan your first few days very carefully because these days are important "getting to know you" days. This period is the time to guide your students in understanding classroom procedures. Keep students busy so that you are free to observe or work with small groups or individuals. Many children will be busy observing you; instead, turn the tables and observe them. Preplanning and advance preparations will create a good foundation on which future plans can be built.

(3) Have you set aside a definite time during the week for thinking, evaluating, and planning?

Many professional novelists and writers complain that it is an effort to sit down and think, that some days ideas just pour forth, but at other times they have not even the glimmer of a thought. Yet most such writers set aside certain hours of the day and force themselves to produce.

Teaching demands thought, investigation, and evaluation of what has been accomplished. This forethought leads to intelligent planning for your students. Provide the time to give thought to academic weaknesses and plan the kind of program that will help strengthen learning ability. If you make a commitment to a definite planning time each week, it may become a habit pattern and become easier with practice.

(4) Do you use your time efficiently?

Teachers come in all sizes and shapes, and with a variety of personalities, drives, and energy levels. Each individual must look for a method of operation that suits his temperament and helps him make the most of the time available.

If you do your best work in the morning, it is best to get to school as early as possible, regardless of what time your school day officially starts. The advantages of arriving early are that (a) you can work in a quiet atmosphere without interruption; (b) you avoid waiting for a turn to use equipment such as duplicating machines and typewriters; (c) you can check audiovisual equipment to see that it is operating efficiently; and (d) you can check on plans for the day and make sure the materials needed for each lesson are available.

If you work best in the afternoon, then preparations might be done after the students leave. Materials can be readied for the following day so that your mornings are not rushed and you can begin teaching in a relaxed manner.

When you dismiss students for recess and lunch, take a few minutes to revise future plans, if necessary, and make your room ready for the next activity. Five or ten minutes here and there, throughout the day, if efficiently used, help to shorten after-school work. It is best to work on these plans before you leave the room; once you relax it is hard to come back to the room before you have to. Another advantage to using a few minutes at a time is that you remember clearly the problems noted during the previous activity, and your plans and preparations will follow through accordingly.

Do not expect to teach, evaluate, plan, and prepare needed materials in the set hours of the school day; expect to do some homework. It is very helpful to be organized so that you know what you have to do and when to do it.

INCORPORATING ALL THE REQUIRED COURSES

Years ago "efficiency experts" designed plans for industrial operations so that each activity flowed into another to ensure that the most work was accomplished in the least time. Today, these men are called industrial engineers. Go back to the original title and think of yourself as an efficiency expert. You have to fit many subjects into a limited period of time. How can you do this efficiently and smoothly?

(1) Are you flexible in your programming?

Not too long ago, some school systems were program oriented. There were definite time slots required for the various subject areas. Fortunately, this rule is no longer true in most of the country. It is now possible to be student oriented and permit a child's needs and interest to dictate the time for shifting to another subject.

Instead of thinking of daily time requirements, develop a weekly time program. For example, if you are teaching a first-grade class and you have allotted fifteen to thirty minutes a day for math, think of using seventy to 150 minutes a week for math. If you need more time to develop a concept, but your daily program does not allow it, try to program that subject for fewer and longer periods of time. One teacher found it difficult to develop the concept of liquid measurement in the short daily time devoted to math. In this group there was a need for many concrete experiences, which took a great deal of time. To meet this problem, she depleted her weekly time allotment in three days and "paid back" the time taken from other subject areas on the last two days of the week when she used the math time for the other subjects. In this way a relaxed atmosphere prevailed because the teacher did not feel the pressure of working against time and permitted the students to enjoy the experiences they were having.

(2) Are you aware of the interrelatedness of all subject areas?

Oral language is being experienced, taught, and learned throughout the day. When the students discuss math problems and answer higher order questions (not the yes-and-no variety), they are expressing themselves orally. Discussions held during social studies periods are other times when pupils speak out and become immersed in the transferrence of thought into clearly expressed ideas. Therefore, scheduling oral language for a definite time is unrealistic because language training is an ongoing activity.

The same is true of reading. Most daily programs provide definite times for reading, but actually children are reading most of the day: They read their assignment directions, their math problems, and do a great deal of reading while doing research for a project.

The skills of computational arithmetic are taught at scheduled times, but math concepts are used quite casually at other times during the day. When goodies are shared, cries of "greater than" and "less than" are heard. "I am bigger than you are" is another familiar statement. Your students are exposed to all the required courses all day, but many are not recognized in their informal guise.

Therefore, if you have to devote more time to a given subject, do not feel guilty if you have to neglect another subject.

While you must plan to teach all the subject areas required for a given grade, the required courses for each day are those the children might need at any given time to accomplish a learning experience. That requirement is the most important of all.

TIME TO WORK WITH INDIVIDUAL CHILDREN

One way to investigate students' problems, if you are in the average classroom of thirty students, is through small group endeavors. However, it is vitally important to work with some students on a one-to-one basis at certain times. This can be done within the classroom setting if you plan for it.

(1) Have you made an assessment of your role as teacher?

Analyze what your job entails and what you really should accomplish. You have many side duties that must be done, but do they need your physical presence all the time? Perhaps you truly fulfill your role when you permit your students to do things for themselves to develop self-reliance.

For example, it is not necessary for you to lead children in the opening exercises of the school day, nor is it important that you call the roll. This can be done by students who have been trained to do these duties. It will take only a few days at the beginning of the year to accomplish these.

Some teachers have attendance cards in envelope pockets on a chart organized like the classroom seating plan. After the class has been seated, the attendance monitor removes the cards of the absentees and records the absences. For younger children, some teachers have an attendance monitor for each group of tables. The monitors record the names of absentees in their group on the chalk board. Another quick attendance check can be accomplished through the use of small envelopes. Each child's name is printed on an envelope and alphabetically placed along the chalk-board ledge. When the children come into the room they pick up their envelope, but in any money they have brought to school, and then file their envelopes behind the appropriate letter found in a dictionary box. Any envelope left on the ledge signifies the absence of that child. The monitor can record this absence on the attendance card or in an attendance book.

If the envelope system is used, the boys' envelopes may be placed in a separate position from the girls' envelopes, thus immediately dividing the group into two smaller groupings. The monitor can arrange the envelopes alphabetically. Zelda will not be crowding Ann when she gets her envelope because she will know that hers is closer to the back part of the room. Four alphabet boxes should be used, two for the boys and two for the girls. If most of the boys' names, say, begin with the letters A through L, there should be fewer letters in the first box. Manipulate the environment and organize a smooth and flowing system that avoids crowding and pushing. This system is preferred by teachers who have to collect lunch or milk money every morning. After the children have filled their envelopes, the teacher can put the box in a safe place so that no one is unnecessarily tempted to have a moral breakdown. It is an easy way to avoid lectures and sermons.

(2) Have you trained your students to get busy as soon as they have completed the morning routines?

It is not necessary to try to brainwash children into blind obedience, even if that could really be done. No matter what you do you will not be able to train your whole group to sit quietly and wait for your signal to begin an activity. It is important to make interesting materials available to the students so they can get involved soon after the opening exercises. In this way you have some extra time for conferences to start a particular child's day with individual attention.

The following are some ideas for student activities during this time:

(a) Put a brain teaser on the board before your students arrive. It could be a long word from which they try to write as many words as they can.

(b) Have them rearrange letters and see how many different words can be made using the same letters—for example, "meat," "team," "mate," "tame."

(c) Write a simple direction on the board leaving out the vowels—for example, "T_k_ _ _t _ m_s_c b_ _ _k. T_rn t_ p_g_ 150." Have them answer a question about something on that page.

(d) Make a chart of a secret code in which letters are written as numerals—for example, A = 1, B = 2, C = 3, and so on. Write an epigram or motto in the numerical code and have the children decode it.

(e) Give the students simple crossword puzzles. After a short learning period children enjoy working on such puzzles, and there are many commercial ones to suit all grade levels. With experience the children can eventually create their own puzzles.

(f) Before the class comes in, write a detailed list of directions for the children to follow—for example:
   1) Help yourself to a sheet of lined paper.
   2) Sign your name in the lower right-hand corner.
   3) Fold your paper lengthwise twice. You should have four columns.
   4) In the first column write as many letters of the alphabet as you can.
   5) In the second column write the name of an animal that begins with the letter on that line.
   6) In the third column write the name of a city beginning with that letter.
   7) In the fourth column write the name of a state or a country beginning with that letter.

(g) Scrambled-word cards can be made up and put in a box from which children can help themselves. The Sunday comics usually have a section of scrambled words which can be cut and mounted on the cards. If you cannot find those, just take words they can already read and mix them up—for example:

(center)   (create)

(h) Duplicate a list of objects and ask the children to arrange them in categories such as clothing, food, toys, tools, or cars.

(i) Give the children a box of job cards on which you have typed math puzzlers—for example:

1) Triple a given recipe.

2) Measure the length and width of room, the height of desk and chair, the width of the door, the width of the chalk board, and so on.

3) Complete sequences:

```
2 ... 3 ... 4 ... 5 ... ... ... ... ...
44 ... 45 ... 46 ... ... ... ... ...
9 ... 8 ... 7 ... ... ... ... ...
6 ... 12 ... 18 ... ... ... ...
52 ... 48 ... 24 ... 20 ... 10 ... ... ... ...
1 ... 3 ... 2 ... 4 ... 3 ... 5 ... ... ... ...
```

(j) Paste maps to stiff cardboard and make jigsaw puzzles.

(k) Using a map of a particular state, ask the student to find the best route to travel from one city to another and determine how many miles it is and how long it will take him to make the trip at a given speed.

These types of activities can be started early in the day and worked on individually whenever the student has spare time. They begin the day in a relaxed and informally busy way and orient the student to a noncompetitive learning atmosphere. Always have answer sheets available for the activities so that each child can find the correct answers.

(3) Have you organized your program to leave time for individual conferences?

There are times during the day when you can organize your students into small groups, with one child assuming the role of teacher. The leader can read to his group or drill his team in spelling, arithmetic facts, or vocabulary. Another group can be involved in a team-tutoring activity. Two children can work together with picture cards that have descriptive words. Because there is a picture, the child can read the word while the other student records it on a small chalk board or on a slate. The reader then becomes the recorder and the other child becomes the reader. An upper-grade student might serve as a teacher aide at given times during the day. It would help some of the slow-learning children to become tutors to the younger students. While teaching them, the older pupil may be strengthening his own skills. He can become a secretary and record the stories that his younger peers composed. Children can help each other learn, but more important is the enjoyment they experience in helping each other.

Try to organize a grouping of classes for the daily physical education period. Two teachers can work with three classes during this activity. This permits the third teacher to have time for an individual conference with one of his students who needs help. Of course, this method needs administrative guidance and cooperation from the other teachers on the staff.

If you think of your students as individuals and not as one large group, you will begin to develop the kinds of activities that will give you time to work with each individual who would benefit from a one-to-one conference. Keep in mind certain factors that help to ensure successful conferences. It is better to schedule short units of time so that children do not get tired of what they are doing. Your involvement might last longer than the interest span of the rest of the class. See to it that your students are very involved in their activities. It helps to schedule time segments with alternatives children can go to if they run out of interest before the activity time is up.

(4) Have you investigated the use of volunteers or paraprofessional aides?

Upon entering a classroom it is not uncommon to see several parent volunteers involved with small groups or working with just one child. Mothers or grandmothers who have spare time enjoy reading stories to children. They can help in recording stories, tutoring a child who needs it, or giving a reassuring pat on the shoulder to help him over a hurdle.

Check into the possibility of recruiting high school seniors to form a club for future teachers. With a few training meetings they can become quite proficient and help children who are working on assignments. It is important to devote one training period to making these assistants aware of the fact that they should not work a child's assignment for him, but just guide him toward answering his own questions. This task will be easier if you have prepared teaching aids for the assistants. For example, if your students are working on computational problems, have individual rulers available which can be used as number-lines or possibly cuisinaire rods or other concrete materials. Before a writing assignment make sure children have dictionaries or boxes with alphabetized dividers available to them. The aides can write needed words and the child can slip the words in the box.

In some schools educational aides have already been trained to work with children, but they will still need your guidance in how best to work with your group. Although it takes time to train people, it is often time well spent because eventually these volunteers and aides free you to work with individual children in an effective way.

TIME TO COMPLETE AND EVALUATE LESSONS

We sometimes think of time as an ogre that acts independently and is constantly interfering with the job at hand. Time moves inexorably forward and we feel we have no control over it. Since time is a constant we cannot change, we must investigate variables that are to some extent under our control.

(1) Do you allow students time to complete their work?

You cannot stop time, but you can plan small learning segments that allow all your students to complete their work. Since each class has a wide range of abilities, this sometimes creates the problem of what to do with the more capable learners who usually complete their work earlier than the others. Some teachers have found it helpful to have stimulating interest areas ready for those who have completed their assignments. (See Chap. 4 for some ideas.) If the majority of the group has finished the work, it is a good idea to have a transitional activity that will allow the stragglers to complete their work too.

Some of the following ideas might be helpful.

(a) Pantomime an action and ask the group to guess what you are doing. Begin with easily recognizable and workaday activities, such as entering a car, driving it, stopping for a red light, and backing it into a parking place. Thread an imaginary needle and pretend it is difficult to do until you put on a pair of glasses. As soon as possible, transfer the pantomime activity to a student. With older children one can add subtleties to the act by pretending to read a book while they try to guess the contents by your facial expressions.

(b) Teach or review a poem. Some students love to recite before the whole class. If some students are shy, send two or three to the front of the room at the same time. This seems to help those who are too bashful to stand alone.

(c) Put some articles on the floor or table, ask a child to leave the room, and remove one of the objects. Upon his return he must name the article that has been removed. The older the group, the more articles should be on view.

(d) An effective transitional activity for the primary grades is for you to sit on a chair in front of the room, beckon to one child, who then exchanges seats with you, both of you tiptoeing to your new places. Continue until everyone has had a turn to sit in teacher's chair. To make it even more interesting, have each child carry a plastic cup full of water. Can they tiptoe without spilling a drop?

These are quiet activities that will enable the slower workers to complete their assignments without pressure to hurry up.

(2) Do you program time for instant evaluation into your teaching unit?

If there is a time lapse between a completed assignment and performance evaluation, the students' learning does not fully benefit from the feedback. A grade of so many right or wrong answers does not help a pupil understand how to correct the problem. Train your students to evaluate their own work by having the answer sheets ready and available. Once the pupil has graded his own paper, the teacher can examine the paper. Impress upon the students the importance of checking which answers were wrong. This act will enable both the student and the teacher to investigate why there was an incorrect answer. Was it due to carelessness because of a desire to rush through the assignment? Is there a missing step that might cause a pupil to have difficulty with a concept? Is the assignment so poorly conceived that the learner has no interest in it and is not motivated to work? The grade a student receives is not as important as the "why's" behind it. It is this type of feedback that provides the teacher an insight into learning problems. With instant evaluation, the problem experienced is fresh in the learner's mind and he might be able to explain his difficulty more readily.

Plan for evaluation time within your directed lesson. If the students have completed their work before instructions, they can evaluate their work as a part of the lesson. If they do their assignment after they leave you, call them back to the reading lesson area and evaluate the work at this time. Other groups can be gainfully occupied with their individual interest such as reading or writing assignments. Even the primary grades can be trained to depend on themselves or get help from their neighbor if they do not know how to write a word. Have picture dictionaries and picture charts of needed nouns, verbs, and adjectives available for them. Also useful are alphabetized word books, in which they will find words they have asked you to write for them in the past. Sometimes a student can use the initial consonant to look up a word if he does not know how to spell it. Alert children to the fact that they know many sound-alike words that can be used as a guide for spelling an unknown word. All of the above ideas can be used in helping students attain some degree of self-reliance, which is developed only when they are given the opportunity of depending on their own abilities and resources.

There are standards important to a smooth transition from assignment to evaluation. Avoid having a line-up of students waiting for you to finish a conference with another student. This line-up is conducive to an exchange of comments which can create a babel of voices. To avoid such confusion, request that each pupil, upon completing his work, write his name on the chalk board and then return to his seat. This is a good time for him to check his work and think about any questions he wants to ask. He might want to resume working on an independent activity that he had not had time to complete. When his name heads the list on the chalk board, he crosses it out and comes to you for his conference. In this type of evaluation period or conference time, you can become aware of weaknesses and make notes of the problems revealed. These notations will help in planning future learning steps for the student.

Rather than bemoan the lack of time for accomplishing the many required tasks, try to manipulate the program, the lesson plan, and the environment so as to efficiently use the time that is available.

TIME FOR RESEARCH INVESTIGATION

One hears of talk of the knowledge explosion. Teachers are told that new facts are being uncovered every day and the information we now have will be obsolete in a short time. The concept of life-long learning can no longer be relegated to a group of esoteric scholars. Today's teacher must not only be aware of social and political events affecting his students, but also of recent curriculum developments, changing teaching methods, and new research findings on the teaching-learning process. In many ways the teacher must be a life-long learner. Obtaining a teaching degree or credential is just the beginning.

It has been said that despite a half century of research and the development of several sophisticated theories, the teacher's classroom activities have been relatively unaffected by what the learning theorist has to say (Jackson, 1968). What are the factors that work against research findings filtering into the classroom? There are at least three.

First, many teachers are also students working toward a higher degree or a new credential. Teaching plus night courses and assignment deadlines do not leave time to read research studies and reports, unless that report is involved in one of the courses.

Secondly, the teaching profession is a demanding one. The constant interaction between teacher and student, and student and student, can create emotional pulls and crises that drain one's energy far more than does any physical activity. By the time the teacher has completed the school day, the planning and paper work that is an adjunct to teaching, and has fulfilled responsibilities and duties of his private life, he is usually too tired to delve into journals and books.

Thirdly, educational psychologists seem to address their findings to other psychologists and couch their writings in esoteric language or drown their findings in statistical results. They complain that teachers want a cookbook recipe of how to teach. What teachers ask for are varied and effective approaches that will help them put into practice the learning theories that have been developed.

The theory has to be brought out of the laboratory and into the frenetic everyday world of the classroom. What can be done to overcome these factors?

(1) Are you research oriented?

It is within your domain to document learning problems and to experiment with different methods that might be used to alleviate these problems. By keeping up with the literature in your own specialization, you will be in a better position to try new procedures and discard practices that have proven unsuccessful.

If you have been successful in adapting a method to a child, write down the nature of the problem and the methods used, including those that were unsuccessful as well as those that worked. Could you ferret out reasons for the failures? What factors were responsible for the success? Write all the details. Your report could be the basis for a study that will investigate your hypothesis in detail using a larger sample than was available to you.

(2) Do you have a professional library section in your school?

In almost all schools there are programs run by the parent teacher association to raise money for the school library. Some of that money might be channeled into buying new professional books and subscribing to education journals that deal with the new findings in the field of education. If your school system has a professional library, the librarian can help you in furnishing a list of new acquisitions and research monographs.

Some teachers personally subscribe to one publication or another. Why not share the wealth and bring in from home those you have read.

(3) Have you tried to organize a monthly seminar for yourself?

Every school has on its agenda a weekly or bimonthly faculty meeting. Why not devote one meeting a month to research reports? The faculty can be divided into a number of committees with each group responsible for a monthly report. Much time can be saved in such a group endeavor. Journals such as the *Review of Educational Research, Elementary School Journal, The Reading Teacher,* and others too numerous to list here are published for educators. Many school systems have a professional library that can be used by the employees of that school system. The teacher of today, like the doctor, must keep up with the advances made in his field. Teachers, in many cases, are sparked and inspired by each other because they share the same problems and are always looking for ways to solve them. Much can be accomplished working in concert with others in your school through shared readings and discussions of how to translate them into the daily routines of the classroom.

An educational psychologist can be invited to speak to the faculty at the beginning of the year. His talk might orient the group to definite areas of investigations, depending on the problems of your particular school. Of course, all of the above ideas have to be broached to your administrator and organized with his approval and guidance. In working with your faculty, you should be aware that not all the teachers will be interested in participating in such a program. However, the fact that meetings are spaced far apart, and that their needs will be the prime topic, might lead to their acceptance. It is worthwhile to try to initiate such a program.

CONSISTENCY IN WHAT YOU
REQUIRE OF CHILDREN

The requirements you set for your students may be thought of as an auxiliary step in helping them learn. Assignments are given to reinforce learning or to provide additional knowledge in a given subject. However, if this step becomes more important than recognizing a problem that is hindering a child's ability to learn, then your demands might be programming your students for failure.

Being consistent is not always a virtue, nor is inconsistency always the wrong attitude to have. A class contains thirty individuals with different interests, abilities, and physical traits. Think of yourself as a tightrope walker whose body sways in order to maintain its equilibrium. You may have certain requirements that are necessary for the smooth functioning of classroom routines, but the demands you made on your students yesterday might be unrealistic today. This fact might be due to inclement weather, preholiday excitement, or even some personal problems that have developed in a child's home. Being consistent in what you ask of children, in reality, does not depend on you.

(1) Is there a way to plan for flexible consistency?

It is not even good policy to be consistent in adhering to a lesson plan. There are times you might become involved in teaching a concept you had not planned on covering that day. To illustrate this point, let us say you were going to teach a new song. You ask your students to define the word "fair," which is mentioned in the lyrics. Instead of requiring that they learn this song, you find yourself sidetracked into a language arts lesson because the pupils were enjoying discussing the different meanings of that word, and this led to a lesson on homonyms. If you were consistent and refused to be swayed from your original lesson plan, you would have lost a wonderful opportunity to expand your students' vocabulary at a time when they were very interested in doing just that. When interest was high you used the opportunity to have an enjoyable learning experience. Rely on children's reaction to your lesson in determining whether you will continue with the objectives for the day.

If you shift your viewpoint from your requirement to an awareness of the child's physical urgencies and intellectual requirements, then you will be able to use a flexible approach that will consistently make you a more successful teacher.

(2) Can you expect consistency in what you require of children?

What you require of them depends to a great extent on their needs at a particular time. There are children whose physical demands are more urgent than those of your other students. A restless child requires more freedom of movement than one who is phlegmatic or more passive. A child with weak kidneys must be free to go to the bathroom at will. These kinds of needs supercede rules and should be discussed with your students so that the group can make plans for these differences.

DO YOU OFTEN FAIL TO REACH YOUR INSTRUCTIONAL OBJECTIVES?

A few years ago, one of the authors watched a group of art students (in an adult art class) working on individual portraits of a live model. One artist had the figure blocked out in a few minutes. A half hour later, the portrait was completed, and the artist glowed with joy because he was first to finish the assignment, and he was very satisfied with the result. Another student spent three hours trying to capture the model's right shoulder. He worked on the front, back, and side view of the right upper arm, trying to portray the underlying musculature in an intricate and subtle manner. When this artist was interrupted because the class was over, he was quite upset because he had not accomplished what he had set out to do.

One teacher might be very demanding of himself and his students. Another might cover all subject matter he had scheduled to do and be satisfied with it, even though his teaching was very superficial and he permitted no deviation from his program. One teacher might be teaching in depth, the other might be shallowly covering a great deal of ground. One teacher might be proud about finishing an entire math workbook, whereas another might feel secure that in what he had covered his students would be proficient. Since the goals and standards of individuals vary, the problem of instructional objectives can only be approached in a general manner.

(1) Are you trying to accomplish too much at a time?

A common failing shared by many beginning teachers is that of "overteaching." In their effort to do everything a teacher manual recommends, they try to cover too much ground in one sitting. The result is student restlessness because of boredom or need for physical movement. If students have stopped listening before you have finished talking, no matter how good your lesson plans are on paper, nothing is being learned. It has often been said that children have a short attention span. Can it be that teachers are boring their students? This is a question that the educator must constantly investigate.

(2) Are your goals realistic?

For years teachers have been admonished to begin teaching at the level at which the child is most comfortable. In their haste to push the pupil ahead, they did not listen enough, nor observe long enough, nor test him adequately to find out his present academic level. As a result, the teacher may complete the required material leaving some students far behind.

When you understand the abilities of your students, your aims will be realistically geared to them. Successful accomplishment of what you set out to do is not important. What is vital is that your students achieve the goal that is geared to their abilities.

MOTIVATING YOURSELF
TO DO AN EFFECTIVE JOB

Motivation is the keystone of any job well done. Before one can do justice to any task, there must be a desire to do it. What are some possible reasons behind the lack of motivation?

(1) Why are you in the teaching profession?

Are you teaching because someone convinced you that it is a good job for you? If teaching is not the profession of your choosing, you must decide for yourself whether there are areas in your work that you do enjoy. Are there enough compensations for you to overcome the things you do not enjoy in teaching? Make a pro-and-con list and see which side has the most entries. If your lack of motivation stems from a dislike of your job, you can either leave the profession or try concentrating on the things you do enjoy about it.

Extrinsic motivations, such as pleasing someone who wanted you to be a teacher, or the advantages of shorter hours and long vacations, will not help you enjoy your work; nor will they help you do an effective job. Concentrate on enjoying children. Do not look at them as receptacles for facts; think of them as a social group of multifaceted individuals who act and react. With every group you will find many gratifying experiences that will help build an inner motivated desire to help children learn and grow.

Are you teaching because you could not decide what to do and therefore chose education? If you had no desire to train for another profession, then perhaps no other field attracted you enough to make you choose it. Consequently, you must assume that *something* in the field of education attracted you to it. Perhaps you enjoy working with people rather than things. If this were not true, you could never have made the choice to teach. In the classroom you are interacting incessantly with thirty or some individuals.

Concentrate on the positive reasons that aided you in your decision to become a teacher. While teaching is a demanding profession, it is also a rewarding one. Which reaction will be dominant depends on your approach to it. Come to it negatively, reluctantly, begrudgingly, and it becomes a frustrating and aggravating job. Students reflect your attitudes. Think of it as an important contribution to a child's growth, and that child will react to your interest and create a glow of accomplishment for himself as well as for you.

(2) Are you doing the same teaching job year after year?

It is easy for one to do things out of habit. Some teachers never change the grade level they are teaching, nor do they try new methods or new pedagogical ideas. They have organized their material and used it over and over again. Without innovations and different approaches, it is easy for the experienced teacher to grow stale; at this point, teaching becomes tasteless and unexciting. One works by rote and habit and barely investigates the differences among students. Materials are more important than children.

While trying to find answers, you may discover innovative ideas that spark new approaches to teaching and learning. You will be exercising your mind and expanding your abilities. Professional growth leads to a sense of accomplishment, which might trigger an inner motivation to do an effective job.

TEACHING SUBJECTS YOU DO NOT LIKE

It is axiomatic that we do not like to do things we do not do well. We avoid subject areas that we do not fully understand and may feel inadequate when exposed to those areas.

(1) Why do you not like a specific subject, or subjects, in the curriculum?

Investigate possible reasons for your dislike. It might be that you missed an important learning experience, which prevented you from ever catching up. This could have caused you to feel insecure in that area. It is possible that your lack of self-confidence made you dread that subject. Even though you know your subject matter in the grade level at which you are teaching, that dread you once felt is still haunting you. By now it has become an emotional reaction that is almost involuntary.

To exorcise this old reaction think of a positive aspect that can come forth from a bad experience. Are you aware of the empathy you have for children who are experiencing difficulty with a subject? An old folk saying goes, "In order to be tender, you have to go through hot water." Often a teacher who himself had a learning problem as a child knows how lost a child can feel when he does not understand a teacher.

Holt (1964) described his neurotic reaction to one learning experience. He came to a music lesson tired after a long and frustrating day. As he began making mistake after mistake, his music teacher began pressuring him to do better. As the tension began building to a high intensity, he suddenly became note-blind. The music before him lost all meaning. Holt used this experience to heighten an awareness in his readers of what children might be experiencing when they are labeled as having word-blindness. These frustrating learning experiences can enrich us as teachers and help to make us more understanding and perceptive people.

(2) Have you tried varied pedagogical techniques?

In the past few years new methodologies have been explored, both in college courses and in in-service training classes. Large city school systems are experimenting with programs of varied techniques. Expose yourself to these innovative ideas and avail yourself of opportunities to visit these schools. Many systems permit their teachers a morning away from their classrooms to visit experimental schools. Try the in-service classes given by your school system. There usually is a stimulating exchange of ideas among the teacher participants, as well as new methods introduced by the leader of the in-service class.

Think of your classroom as a laboratory and experiment with new approaches. Which method makes the children respond most enthusiastically? Do they perk up and tune you in when you use a method that is different? Is there a difference between the reaction you get from the slower learning group than from the faster group? A fresh approach will make you more enthusiastic, which will be communicated to your students, which in turn might make the subject matter more exciting to teach.

One of the comparatively new and emerging ideas is that of team teaching. If you have a favorite subject and your neighboring teacher is talented in another, why don't you teach your favorite subjects to each others' classes? Of course, this idea must be cleared by your administrator and done with his approval.

If team teaching is not feasible in your particular situation, ask for fresh ideas from your fellow teachers. You might be surprised to discover how many teachers will not only share some of their techniques but will also be gratified that you thought enough of their teaching ability to ask them for advice. Especially in large school systems, where many expert, dedicated teachers are obscured by the large numbers of people, your request for unofficial help from them might be the only commendation they get. You, on the other hand, will benefit by learning a technique that actually works with the students of your particular school, not just for a hypothetical school population.

Our theme is that you should not simply stand pat with your likes and dislikes. It is far more rewarding to search for answers to a problem than to just "push through" the days feeling frustrated or bored. Your children deserve more and so do you.

HANDLING CLERICAL WORK

At certain times during the year a teacher can be swamped by teaching-related clerical work which must be done outside of the teaching schedule. However, most of this work is expected and comes as no surprise. Therefore, you can plan in advance to space the effort so that you can avoid fighting mounds of work and imminent deadlines at the same time.

(1) Do you complete each clerical job as it arises?

Unfortunately, there is never enough time to do all the work you should do, so there is a tendency to put off the jobs that are due at a later date. To avoid a last-minute upsurge, try planning short units of work time. At the beginning of the semester spend fifteen minutes a day filling out the cumulative record cards, attendance cards, and health cards. If you are concerned about possible future class reorganizations in which your group might be shifted to another teacher, just fill in your name in pencil. The vital statistics will be the same. The few minutes you need for this chore can be taken from your lunch period, recess time, or after school. Another reason for short daily periods is that you do not permit yourself to tire, and thus, you avoid many mistakes that can occur when you are fatigued or pressured to get your records in at a certain time.

Attendance registers need not be ignored until the last week of the month. Names can be entered at the beginning of the month, and attendance can be written in each day or at the end of the week. Many schools permit teachers to enter the names of their students once every two months. Names on the left side of the book suffice for two pages.

Report cards are usually due every ten weeks. Try to clear your other work in advance so that you have time for this job. Not only is report-card work a time-consuming task; it calls for decisions that demand much forethought and insightful reasoning. The records you keep of test marks are not the only criterion to use; you must stop to think, consider, and debate when assigning a grade. These decisions take more time than you realize. However, since these are due at definite and fixed times, you can plan in advance.

(2) Do you use the week before school starts and the months before school ends to get some clerical work out of the way?

Some teachers use that period to write long-term plans for their class, although they do not know all the problems of the group they will have. However, requests for films, filmstrips, and other audiovisual materials can be organized on a yearly basis. Before school starts, you have the time to go through audiovisual manuals and become familiar with the materials available. As you plan for long-term goals, you can enter the names and order numbers of the materials that suit your program needs next to the subject matter to be covered. Even if changes are necessary, you will still have most of your needs tabulated.

Two months before the end of the school year is a good time to begin entering the closing remarks on each child's cumulative record card. By this time you know your student's abilities and are well aware of the recommendations you intend to write. You know the ending date of the school year and you can begin to enter the names of the readers and social studies units they have covered, thus leaving time for the final report-card deliberations.

Long-range plans are used as guideposts, not as fixed goals. They can be revised, altered, and changed to suit your students. These plans help you preplan, and preplanning gives you extra time for clerical work, which otherwise can pile up.

CONSTANT INTERRUPTIONS

Many kinds of interruptions can plague the classroom teacher, but with some forethought each type might be avoided or at least minimized.

Suppose you have been working with your class and have just gotten their full attention. They are totally interested and absorbed when there is a buzz from the office. All the children shout out, "The buzzer! The buzzer!" The office monitor gets up and goes off to get the message and the teacher asks, "Now where was I?" A magic moment, a carefully built-up interest in a concept is spoiled. It could be an intercom system that ruins a lesson, or a note from another teacher sent by messenger. No matter what kind of interruption, it can be an annoying, frustrating experience for any teacher.

Can these interruptions be avoided completely? It is doubtful whether any organization can operate without emergencies arising, and these emergencies do cause interruptions. However, interruptions owing to other causes can be avoided. Teachers should discuss this problem at a faculty meeting. Together with the administrator they can work out a system of priorities. An emergency must be taken care of immediately, but others can wait for a more opportune moment. It may take ten or fifteen minutes for the class program to get into full swing. An interruption during these initial minutes will not destroy moods or intrude at a crucial time. The few minutes before dismissal for recess, lunch, and at the end of the day will not cause havoc with a program. A teacher can be notified in advance which of his children are to be examined by the nurse or school doctor and can have them leave quietly at a definite time. A ruling applicable to all teachers—that no last-minute requests are to be made of each other while class is in session—would cut out irrelevant messages during the day. There are enough interruptions from the students themselves that can break into a learning experience without any help from the outside (see Jackson, 1968).

It is not unusual for a parent to look into the room, apologize to the teacher for breaking in but his child forgot his lunch; or the parent overslept and couldn't get the lunch ready in time and may he just give Mary her lunchbox? The teacher smiles and says, "Of course," though he might be inwardly seething because a trend of thought was destroyed and an attentive period was broken. The whole class waits while Mary walks over to her mother, has a whispered conversation with her, puts her lunch away, and returns to her seat. In the meantime whispered conversations are being exchanged. Sometimes the teacher cannot recapture the attention of the class to the same degree it was before. Would it not be better to have late lunches delivered to the office where the children can pick them up later?

A student is late. All work stops while the teacher reprimands the late-comer and then gives him an individual assignment. Again there are distracting comments from other pupils, which means more time is wasted. Have you tried to inculcate a late-comer routine? Make it a rule, for example, that if a tardy child hears the class reciting the pledge of allegiance or singing the anthem, he is to wait outside until the class is finished before he can come in to put away his things. If the group has started work, one person appointed by you can show the late arrival what the assignment is. Another method is to have the late-comer go to a special area where a directions card will instruct him what to do: older children can write the reason for their tardiness, younger children can wait quietly for a break before rejoining the group.

Discuss tardiness routines at the beginning of the semester, so that children know what to do when they arrive after the classroom routines have started. Save reprimands for your tardy students for a time that will not cut into the learning of those who do come on time.

Children can be trained to follow routines, especially if the reason for them is made understandable. In other words, teachers and students must think together, plan together, and set the procedures that will help to eliminate as many unnecessary interruptions as possible.

CASE INCIDENTS

Case incident 1: Destructive discipline

Mrs. Jackson was a strict disciplinarian. She taught in a second-grade class and she believed that second-graders should be treated in an adultlike manner. Her class behaved well and respected her judgment, and she in turn respected them. She believed in being honest with them, and therefore would not give a student a B+ or A– if they were close to the A range, or a C+ or a B– if they were close to the B range. Instead, she gave the children the grades that she thought they deserved—A, B, C, D, F; no +'s or –'s. She believed she was helping her children by showing them that they did not complete the lesson correctly. However, Mrs. Jackson was always too busy to go over any errors, so repetition of these same errors was frequent.

Mrs. Jackson would give her class a penmanship exercise and watch each child proudly make his marks upon the paper. But the next day there were many looks of dismay because many students had gotten back F papers. Mrs. Jackson went around the room telling each student that improvement was needed and more practice would help.

Shortly after report cards were sent home, Mrs. Jackson received a call from a distraught mother who could not understand why her daughter's report-card grades were so poor when all her assignment papers had received good marks.

"Perhaps Mary only brings home the A and B papers," said Mrs. Jackson. "I'll have a talk with her."

When she talked to Mary, her suspicions were confirmed: Mary had indeed brought home only the good papers, not the F papers.

"Mary, I can't understand you," Mrs. Jackson said. "I hand back all your papers. Why don't you correct them and try again? Practice makes perfect, you know."

"Why should I try?" replied Mary. "All I ever get is F's anyway!"

Discussion Questions. What is the purpose of evaluation? How is evaluation most effectively accomplished in the elementary school? What is Mary telling Mrs. Jackson? What steps can Mrs. Jackson take to help Mary?

STUDENT NOTES

Case incident 2: *"Get it together"*

Mrs. Morris, experiencing her first teaching assignment, complained to a fellow teacher that she was having a very difficult time:

"Something must always be planned or the children's attention just wanders away. I know I do not have to follow my schedule exactly, but I must know where I am going. This means a lot of preparation of lessons, dittos, and materials for motivation. There is hardly time during the school hours to worry about this, so I take it home to do. Besides this work, I spend hours every night correcting papers. During my breaks at school, I run off the dittos, and since each child uses about three dittos I spend my coffee-break time running off the materials for each day's work.

"Even though I work hard, I know the principal is annoyed with me because my room environment leaves much to be desired. But when can I find time to do everything that needs to be done? Should I neglect the children's work and concentrate on bulletin boards?

"My husband is upset with me because he thinks I'm spending too much time on my job. But without this extensive outside preparation I can't have everything done!"

Discussion Questions.   What are time-saving methods Mrs. Morris can use? How can she avoid some of her clerical work? Is it necessary for a teacher to give up all the breaks in the day's routine? How can a teacher prevent conflict among the many roles she plays (of wife, teacher, etc.)?

STUDENT NOTES

Case incident 3: Flexibility without flaccidity

Mrs. Smith, a fourth-grade teacher in an upper-middle-class section of a large city, believed that much of her class's motivation was gone. After four weeks of school her students did not seem as interested in learning as they had at the beginning of the year. Then they had come to school full of questions and interested in many things. Now they seemed to be doing all the assignments without much "spark."

A typical Monday started as follows:

"John," Mrs. Smith asked, "will you please start current events today?"

"Yes, Mrs. Smith, but I would like to show everyone some of the new rocks I found at the river."

"Well, John, I think that can wait for another time."

This had happened often before when children had things to share and there was a shortage of time. Later, the class was involved with its math. For the first time in days the classroom was quiet and thoughtful. There had been some trouble lately with the math. The children seemed very pressured and pushed by it. That day Mrs. Smith was trying new books. At 11:00 the class was still concentrating. At about 11:05 Mrs. Smith asked the class to hand in the papers and close their books.

Jane asked, "Can I work on this just a little longer?"

Mrs. Smith answered, "No, we have to move on today."

On another day the class watched a social studies movie. Usually these weekly movies took about forty-five minutes; however, this one took an hour and twenty minutes. As a result there was only a half hour left for math.

"Mrs. Smith," Andy said, "can we have our music now and our math after lunch so we'll have more time to work on it?"

"No, Andy," Mrs. Smith answered, "we will have too much to do after lunch."

Discussion Questions. How could Mrs. Smith be more flexible in her scheduling? Can a teacher be too flexible in her programming? How could Mrs. Smith incorporate the students' suggestions into her program?

STUDENT NOTES

Case incident 4: *Teacher's program versus student's needs*

Mrs. Benson had been teaching for five years, all of it in the first grade, although she had always wanted to teach fourth or fifth grade. Finally, because of a rapid turnover in teachers, she found herself teaching a fifth-grade class. After six months she felt quite frustrated but was more than anxious to go on. Life in first grade, she discovered, was very different from that in fifth grade.

She discussed her problems with a fellow teacher at the beginning of the second semester:

"I seem to be doing more and more planning and preparation now. I used to be able to work out a lesson plan for a week in a matter of a few hours. Now, what I want to accomplish in one day, my students get done in half the time. I don't want to overload them with a lot of work, but at the same time I don't want them to be bored."

Her friend, a first-grade teacher herself, suggested a few activities. "You might fill in the time with short games. Or let them have independent reading. I hear [another fifth-grade teacher] gives his class a lot of independent reading."

Mrs. Benson rejected the idea of playing games, since she knew only first-grade games; however, she did decide to try an hour of independent reading. The problem was, what would they read? The subject matter differed immensely from first grade.

In one social studies period, she read aloud to the students different stories about the colonists and their life in the New World. There was no class discussion because she wanted to get through as many stories as possible in the allotted time. She noticed many students seemed uninterested and paid her little attention, and she wondered why. To her the stories were well written and informative, and she could not understand why they did not listen to her. She spent more time with the colonists than she meant to, and as a result skipped the science lessons, although it did not bother her since she disliked science.

She always felt it was important to work individually with each child, but more times than not she did not talk to half of her students alone. She began to fill in all the extra time that she had started with in order to try to complete all the subjects prescribed for that semester. First, she took away the hour of "independent reading," so that she could squeeze in a few more spelling words and math problems. Later, as she became more time conscious, she deliberately ignored class discussions that did not pertain to what they were studying at the moment. As a result, at the end of the day she felt a real sense of accomplishment, since she had no more "empty" time.

At the end of the semester she talked again with her friend: "You know, I finally learned to use time constructively; there are no wasted time periods now. But I just wish the kids were more involved in what we do. I wonder why they aren't. Maybe it's just this class, and my next fifth grade will be more responsive."

Discussion Questions. Why do you think Mrs. Benson did not plan enough activities for her new class of fifth graders? Was she equating the work of first graders with fifth graders? What could she do concerning lesson plans? Can you diagnose why her students were uninvolved and less responsive in class? Should she have given the students free reading time? Should she have stuck with it? Who might have been a better person to discuss her problems with and why? Is discussion of topics unrelated to matters being studied good or bad? Should Mrs. Benson have allowed time for such discussions, and what might have she accomplished if she had? Should she return to first-grade teaching? Why or why not?

Case incident 5: Observations and recordings

Many education textbooks emphasize the importance of providing for individual differences in instruction. A good way to learn about a student's strengths and weaknesses is to look at his cumulative record maintained in each school. This record usually includes standardized test scores—particularly IQ and achievement test scores—grades in various subjects, and evaluations by previous teachers. But teachers do not always agree how such information should be used, as the following conversation illustrates:

Mr. Jones: I have to go to the office this afternoon to check Billy Grave's cumulative record. I just don't seem to be able to reach him. I think I need to know more about his past.

Mr. Smith: I realize that teachers like to have such information, but I never check those records. I feel that teachers should make up their own mind about students and not rely on the opinions of others.

Mr. Jones: But what about the test scores? Don't they give you accurate information about student abilities?

Mr. Smith: I don't think so.

Mr. Jones: Well, last year in the educational psychology course I took they said that most standardized tests given in school have high validity and reliability.

Mr. Smith: Well, my tests in high school were supposed to predict how well I would do in college, and they didn't. I know many cases where test scores were meaningless. So why use them? Why form opinions about a student's ability from test scores when the scores could be inaccurate? Why let the biases of other teachers influence your opinion?

Discussion Questions. Why do problems occur when teachers analyze cumulative records? Who is at fault, the records or the teachers? Should these records be neglected? Why do schools keep these records? How can they best be used? What is the difference between validity and reliability of test scores? Are there other factors regarding testing which should be considered when analyzing test scores? What advice do you have for Mr. Jones?

STUDENT NOTES

Case incident 6: Teacher responsibility

Mr. Jans was a member of a committee that trained and assigned volunteer aides to work in a one-to-one relationship with students needing help in a particular subject. It was an important committee because it had been shown that the program the previous year helped many students who might otherwise have fallen behind in their work. The teachers and volunteers met one hour each week and each teacher was responsible for training three aides.

Being conscientious, Mr. Jans never missed a meeting, but Mrs. Foster, the committee chairman, often did. And each time that she missed a meeting, her volunteer aides were assigned to other groups. Resentful, the teachers asked her to come more regularly—to which she answered that her first duty was to her family and not to an extracurricular duty for which she was not being paid.

Everyone on the staff was reluctant to report her to the principal and yet they wanted her to be responsible for her share or else resign. She made no move to do either. No one had a solution to the problem except to complain among themselves.

Discussion Questions. What are some of the problems that occur in committee work? From your own experiences in committee work, do you feel that much of the work could best be accomplished by individuals? Suppose Mr. Jans believed that his role in an effective volunteer program would help his chances of a promotion in the district. How should he handle this situation? Speak to Mrs. Foster? Speak to the principal? Do the work himself? Complain to other faculty members?

STUDENT NOTES

Chapter Four

ORGANIZING FOR INSTRUCTION

The effective teacher is one who determines the level of a child's development, decides how he learns best, and helps him achieve at his own rate. To accomplish these goals, you must realize that there are many different ways to organize a class for instruction. This organization is important in solving many instructional problems.

HELPING CHILDREN LEARN TO THINK

One of the most frustrating experiences a teacher encounters is that of getting an entirely different result from the one planned for in the objectives of a given lesson. Sometimes the result is so distressingly different that it is as if he had never presented a lesson at all.

For example, one teacher spent a great deal of time with his first-grade students in developing the concept of beginning consonants. He used pictures, games, and songs to show the students all the different words that begin with the letter "m." But when he tried to elicit from the children words beginning with that letter, some of the responses were "house," "ball," and "girl." This type of experience leads to the common cry of teachers, "Why don't they think before they answer?" To answer this question we must ask other questions that might help diagnose the problem.

(1) Are you assuming the pupils have acquired the necessary prerequisite capabilities?

Many teachers forget to ascertain whether their students are prepared to proceed with the learning of new material—that is, whether they already possess the prerequisite capabilities or knowledge needed to deal with this new learning. Gagné (1970) found that students are more likely to learn some activity or knowledge when they have previously learned the prerequisite capabilities associated with the learning task, and numerous research studies have supported this conclusion. Weigand (1969) found that in one group thirty out of thirty-one students could not find the solution to a problem presented, but after investigators ascertained which prerequisite skills were needed and instructed the students in them, nine out of ten were able to solve it.

Gagné has developed a model proposing the existence of eight different types of learning, ranging from simple to complex. Success in one type of learning, he believes, is dependent upon prerequisite knowledge of lower types of learning. For example, if problem-solving capabilities are desired, one must first learn certain principles. But before he learns those principles, he must learn specific concepts; and prior to learning concepts he must learn specific associations or facts and discriminate them from each other. Gagné continues this analysis until he reaches the most basic elements in a learning task. The hierarchical model based on a description by Gagné (1965, pp. 58-61), with an example of a learning structure for the basic skills of reading (Gagné, 1965, p. 201), is shown in Figure 3.

You can use Gagné's task-analysis approach to teaching by developing learning hierarchies—routes for learning—when you plan your lessons. If you delineate an entire set of capabilities which the student needs to learn before he can understand a given concept or principle, you are more likely to develop a more effective instructional program. The following situation illustrates the importance of assessing prerequisite skills.

Miss Smith asked a second-grade group of children to listen to a word and then tell her if the consonant "l" was a beginning, middle, or final consonant. The response from them was very poor. In reviewing her plans, Miss Smith decided that she might not have given enough examples of each consonant placement, but even this repetitious approach did not improve their responses. The mystery went unsolved until one day while teaching music she asked the children what the final words in the lines were and discovered they did not understand what "final" meant. Some, indeed, did not understand the concept of "beginningness," which she had assumed they knew.

In diagnosing the problem, Miss Smith decided that her group needed very concrete examples of even the most basic concepts, and planned accordingly. Showing her students three milk cartons stapled together like a partitioned shelf and a small ball, she put the ball in the first box and said, "This is the beginning box in this row of boxes." Then she transferred the ball into the middle and final boxes, telling the children exactly what she was doing. She then asked them to participate by putting the ball in specific boxes. Later, when she again taught placement of consonants, the lesson went very smoothly.

When children are not responding, there may be many reasons. The teacher must be alert to look for the possible causes. Again, often the cause is related to the fact that the teacher assumes the students understand all the necessary prerequisites.

Description of Types of Learning

A Learning Structure
for Basic Skills of Reading

Type 8—Problem-Solving
Involves thinking skills; combinations of
two or more principles to arrive at a
unique solution.

Type 7—Principle Learning
Acquisition of a clear understanding (not
rote learning) of statements relating two
or more concepts in the manner of "If A,
then B."

Principles:
Organization of
paragraphs and
larger units
Order of English
expression

Type 6—Concept Learning
A common classifying response is
made to groups of objects, events, or
ideas, the individual members of which
appear to be dissimilar.

Concepts:
Printed nouns, verbs,
prepositions,
connectives

Type 5—Multiple Discriminations
Learning to discriminate among many
similar-appearing stimuli and to respond
to them in as many different ways.

*Multiple
discriminations:*
Distinguishing
similar words

Concepts:
Stimuli of oral
speech

Type 4—Verbal Association
Learning to link combinations of words
as stimuli with words as responses.
Language also provides the basis for
implicit 1 links called mediators.

Verbal sequences:
Recognition of
printed words

Type 3—Chaining
Learning to link a chain of two or more
stimulus-response connections.

Chaining:
Recognition of
printed letters by
sound

Chaining:
Oral production of
words

Type 2—Stimulus-Response Learning
The acquisition of precise connections
between a given response and a
discriminated stimulus.

Ss→R learning:
Language sounds

Ss→R learning:
Simple words

Type 1—Signal Learning
The learning of a general, diffuse response
to a signal as in classical conditioning. It
is not clear that Type 1 is a prerequisite
for Type 2.

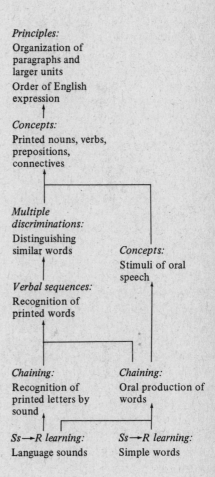

Figure 3. Gagné's hierarchical model of learning with an example of a learning structure for basic skills of readings. (From *Educational Psychology: Instruction and Behavior Change* by Di Vesta, F., and Thompson, G. Copyright © 1970. By permission of Appleton-Century-Crofts, Educational Division, Meredith Corporation.)

(2) Are you assuming all students have the same ability to understand a given concept?

Teachers are often disturbed that some students in their class do not appear to grasp concepts as quickly as other students. The Swiss psychologist Piaget offers a possible explanation.

Piaget believes children proceed through various stages of intellectual development. In each stage they acquire different intellectual structures or abilities which allow them to deal with more complex subject matter. The system of thought present in childhood (ages 6-7 to about 10-11) is quite different from that present in adolescence, after age 11 (Elkind, 1968).

The young child is limited by the stimuli presented to him (Inhelder and Piaget, 1958); the only means he has of organizing his thinking are perceptual. When he sees two small glasses of the same size and shape filled with the same amount of water, then sees the water from one glass poured into a third glass that is taller and narrower, he tends to conclude that the quantity of water has changed—that the third glass contains more water than the first because "it is higher." He says this even though he readily admits that no water has been added or removed.

Piaget found that until the age of 6 or 7, a child's thinking is not deductive or inductive, but *trans*ductive. Deduction is reasoning from the general to the specific—for example, if we assume that all children are good, and we see a specific child, we deduce that he is good. Induction is reasoning from the specific to the general—if we meet several good children, we could conclude that all children are good. But according to Piaget the child in the first or second grade is often thinking somewhere in between, moving from particular to particular without touching on the general. These children see some relationship between particular instances when there is none (Ginsburg and Opper, 1969).

The child who walks through the forest not knowing if he sees a succession of turtles or the same one reappearing is thinking transductively. Piaget (1952, p. 232) gave as one example the remark of his daughter when she failed to take a nap one afternoon: "I haven't had my nap, so it isn't afternoon." Often children this age see relationships between particular instances such that if A causes B, then B causes A. This type of thinking is a limitation in certain learning situations.

As the child becomes older he acquires additional intellectual abilities to solve problems he could not solve previously. However, it is not until he becomes about 11 years old that he is able to think abstractly. Then he can deal with verbal propositions and can engage in combinatorial thinking—the ability to consider all the possible combinations within a system while attempting to find a solution to a problem.

Unless the teacher is aware of the intellectual development of children, he can use the finest textbooks to develop interesting and stimulating lessons, and still fail to reach a majority of his students. If children do not have the abilities to understand the presented material, learning will not occur.

A major implication of Piaget's theory is that the most effective learning takes place when the instructor matches the complexity of the subject matter to the cognitive development of his students, keeping in mind that not all the students in a class may be at the same point in their intellectual development.

After working with teachers in the development of a science curriculum, Karpus (1964, p. 113) stated:

You will probably all agree that there is a transition between children's preoperational thinking at kindergarten age and some of their thinking in terms of propositions when pupils leave elementary school at twelve or so. It seems to me that in general this transition in children's thinking is not recognized by present educational practice in the United States. Teachers with whom I have been in contact have not seemed to be aware that there is such a change taking place and I would say that most instruction above the kindergarten takes place on what one might call the formal level. As an unfortunate consequence of this fact many students never understand the intent of instruction and become dissatisfied with school by the time they are fourteen or sixteen.

Piaget's theory has more implications for teaching, but it is impossible to do justice to his work here. See the Bibliography at the end of the book for further reading.

(3) Have you analyzed your questioning skills?

Gall (1970) found consistent results in reviewing studies on teachers' questioning practices. About 60 percent of teachers' questions require students to recall facts, about 20 percent require them to think, and the remaining 20 percent are procedural questions. The type and quality of thinking in the classroom may be strongly influenced by the teacher's behavior. Thus, if you consistently ask only factual-type questions in class, the chances are great that your students will respond with the same type of questions.

Recently, Bloom's *Taxonomy of Educational Objectives* (1956) has been used to develop guidelines for formulating questions and instructional objectives. Bloom identified six categories of thinking which can be related to all intellectual objectives in education. Table 1 describes these categories.

Sanders (1966) has used the Bloom taxonomy to train teachers in how to vary the questions they ask students in social studies. He believes that a teacher can improve the quality of thinking in the classroom by carefully planning to ask questions at all levels of the taxonomy. The teacher might ask, "Am I offering all appropriate intellectual experiences or am I overemphasizing some and neglecting others?" With this guideline, the teacher often can be made more sensitive to the opportunities for many different kinds of thinking. In some instances, the teacher may decide to ask a question on the *knowledge* level—for example, "What is the largest city in Missouri?" However, he may want to increase the level of thinking by asking a question at the *application* level—for example, "How would you go about solving the smog problem in Los Angeles?"

Or he may ask one at the *evaluation* level—for example, "How effective has the governor been in improving education in the state?"

Another way to improve the quality of student answers is through probing questions that go beyond the usually superficial first answer. Borg *et al.* (1970, p. 61) discussed four types of probing questions studied by researchers at Stanford University (McDonald and Allen, 1967):

1. Seeking further clarification.—This technique elicits more information and meaning from the pupil; e.g., "What do you mean?" "Can you explain that further?"

Table 1. Major Categories in the Cognitive Domain of the Taxonomy
of Educational Objectives (Bloom, 1956)

Descriptions of the Major Categories in the Cognitive Domain

I. Knowledge. Knowledge is defined as the remembering of previously learned material. This may involve the recall of a wide range of material, from specific facts to complete theories, but all that is required is the bringing to mind of the appropriate information. Knowledge represents the lowest level of learning outcomes in the cognitive domain.

II. Comprehension. Comprehension is defined as the ability to grasp the meaning of material. This may be shown by translating material from one form to another (words to numbers), by interpreting material (explaining or summarizing), and by estimating future trends (predicting consequences or effects). These learning outcomes go one step beyond the simple remembering of material, and represent the lowest level of understanding.

III. Application. Application refers to the ability to use learned material in new and concrete situations. This may include the application of such things as rules, methods, concepts, principles, laws, and theories. Learning outcomes in this area require a higher level of understanding than those under comprehension.

IV. Analysis. Analysis refers to the ability to break down material into its component parts so that its organizational structure may be understood. This may include the identification of the parts, analysis of the relationships between parts, and recognition of the organizational principles involved. Learning outcomes here represent a higher intellectual level than comprehension and application because they require an understanding of both the content and the structural form of the material.

V. Synthesis. Synthesis refers to the ability to put parts together to form a new whole. This may involve the production of a unique communication (theme or speech), a plan of operations (research proposal), or a set of abstract relations (scheme for classifying information). Learning outcomes in this area stress creative behaviors, with major emphasis on the formulation of *new* patterns or structures.

VI. Evaluation. Evaluation is concerned with the ability to judge the value of material (statement, novel, poem, research report) for a given purpose. The judgments are to be based on definite criteria. These may be internal criteria (organization) or external criteria (relevance to the purpose) and the student may determine the criteria or be given them. Learning outcomes in this area are highest in the cognitive hierarchy because they contain elements of all of the other categories, plus conscious value judgments based on clearly defined criteria.

Source: *Stating Behavioral Objectives for Classroom Instruction* by Gronlund, N.
Copyright 1970. By permission of The Macmillan Company.

2. Increasing student critical awareness.—This technique elicits a rationale for the initial answer; e.g., "What are you assuming here?" "Why do you think that is so?"

3. Refocusing the student's response.—This technique directs the pupil's attention to a related issue if he has given an acceptable first response; e.g., "How does this relate to . . . ?" "Can you take it from there and tie it in to . . . ?"

4. Prompting.—This technique is used when the pupil has given a poor initial response to the teacher's question; e.g., "I don't know," or "I'm not sure." Prompting gives the pupil a hint to help him answer the question rather than simply giving him the answer. For example, if he cannot answer the question, "Why is it that this object sinks in water but the other one does not?" the teacher might offer a prompt, "Does the reason have something to do with the size or mass of the object?"

Finally, be sure to provide pupils with enough time to answer a question. A three- or four-second pause may seem a long time to the impatient teacher, but the child should not be afraid the teacher will call on someone who is wildly waving his hand if he does not immediately answer. If he does not answer soon enough to please you, tell him that you will give him more time and will come back to him.

If you have been complaining about the quality of thinking in your classroom, try analyzing the type and quality of questions you have been asking as one possibility in the diagnosis of the problem.

(4) Have you tried some different exercises?

The following ideas are some ways of helping young children develop the needed background for thinking. These ideas can be made more sophisticated for older students.

a) Teach students to pay attention to detail by showing them incomplete pictures and asking what is missing—for example, the leg of a table, the ear of a bunny, the handle of a kettle. For older students use a more elaborate picture such as a television antenna, omitting a small item that will take a concentrated effort to discover. Looking for hidden objects in a picture is another form of looking for a detail which all ages enjoy.

b) Train children in the skill of classification. An important step in inductive reasoning is that of generalizing. For young children, have them cut pictures out of magazines and paste them on a piece of paper that has several labeled columns, such as toys, food, clothing. With older children you can give lists of words to be put in the proper column, such as those words used in different jobs or professions, types of tools, or terms used in physics, biology, and chemistry. The level of sophistication depends on the needs of your groups.

c) Sequencing your memory can help you find lost objects or solve other problems. Sequencing a series of events can help you focus your thinking and discover the cause of an effect. It sharpens one's ability to do "if-then" reasoning. For the very young you can use three pictures of an apple, arranged in sequence: an uneaten apple, a half-eaten one, and a core. There are commercial pictures available of sequences, ranging from simple story ideas to more complex for higher grades. Comic strips with action pictures and no words can be mounted on heavy cardboard or chip board; covered with clear contact paper, they will last through many a semester. Sentences from stories that have been read can also be used. Begin by asking the students questions about a story they have just read. Then take three sentences from the story, put them into incorrect sequence, and ask the children to help rearrange the sentences so that they read the story just the way it happened. Eventually, you can use many more sentences.

d) Tell simple stories with illogical endings and ask what is wrong with them. You can make these up without much difficulty. (For example: the boy put on his pants over his head . . . The newborn baby said "Hello" to his brother . . . It rained all day that night . . . He ran so fast it took him an hour to run one block.)

e) Have problem-solving discussions. While there might be different ways to solve problems, some prove to be more efficient than others. (For example: Which solution is best if you lose your sweater? To go home crying because you'll get a spanking? To go around school looking for it? To go to the lost-and-found department.) This type of reasoning may help stimulate alternative solutions to various problems.

f) Ask children to choose the best title for a story. This will later lead to the concept of a story's main idea. For young students, begin with questions asking what the story is about—for example, "What happened to a boy?" Start with the very obvious and gradually lead children to find main themes, main characters, and so on.

g) In the upper grades you can introduce students to the type of thinking that goes "circle is to oval as orange is to. . . ." In primary grades you can begin such reasoning with the simplest of sentences and give them three choices—for example: "Shoe is to foot as hat is to (mother, beautiful, head)." "Apple is to tree as egg is to (carton, hen, barn)." Just as you can use auditory perception for reading readiness, you can also use it when introducing a prerequisite thinking skill. Let students hear it first, then work on the concept using visual aids, group and individual participation, and finally written exercises.

HELPING CHILDREN LISTEN

Have you ever experienced listening to a lecture and then, unaware of even having made the transition, suddenly realized you were daydreaming or thinking about some chores you had to do? One often does not know why his attention wanders.

But as a teacher, you know that an inattentive student might miss an important concept, and thus you should investigate possible causes for it in order to avoid incomplete understandings by the students and frustration by the teacher.

(1) Are you talking too much?

Amidon and Flanders (1967) investigated the verbal interaction between teacher and students and discovered what they called the "two-thirds rule" of the classroom—that is, two-thirds of the time, the teacher does the talking. Is it because verbal people go into teaching, or do people become more talkative because they have a captive audience? This has not been scientifically investigated. What should be investigated is: how much talking do you do?

a) Diagnose your own classroom verbal behavior. Play a tape recorder part of the school day and then listen to how you teach. If you hear your voice most of the time, it is probable that many of your students stopped listening before you finished lecturing.

b) Try to plan your lessons so that there is audience participation. Older children can be grouped in committees whose members give lectures in the form of reports while the others participate in discussions following the reports. Here your best role is that of guide and moderator, not lecturer. With younger children, insert small doses of needed information, then question them to get feedback of what they absorbed and whether they achieved the behavioral objectives of the particular lesson. The important goal is for the children to actively participate in any ongoing experience. Sometimes it is difficult to tell whether your pupils are listening; you may mistake a student's intense look for avid attention. However, you know students are listening when there is much individual participation.

c) Get immediate feedback. A common error many teachers make is to repeat what they were saying several times. Miss Smith gave her students directions and then asked if there were any questions. No one had questions to ask, so the children were told to get to work. No sooner had Miss Smith finished speaking when a few children raised their hands to ask questions that had been answered when the directions were given. After lecturing on the importance of listening, she repeated the directions. Since her students knew Miss Smith would repeat the directions, listening for details became a desultory effort.

   A good rule to follow is to give directions with ample illustrations and then ask for immediate feedback from a random sampling. For example, first ask John to repeat what you said, then turn to Mary and ask her to repeat what the group is to do. There are three reasons why the method is effective: First, students will listen because they are not sure who will be called to repeat what teacher said. Second, the teacher finds out whether the instructions were understood or whether there is a need for more specific details. Finally, some students hear their own peers better than they hear the teacher. For instance, in teaching her class a song, Mrs. Marsh found Jimmy had difficulty singing the starting tone on key and could not hear it when Mrs. Marsh (who had true pitch) sang it or when it was played on song bells. But when Mrs. Marsh asked Andy, who was sitting next to Jimmy, to help, Jimmy was able to mimic Andy's voice.

(2) Do you make sure you have the students' attention before you begin to speak?

Many lecturers will stand quietly until their audience quiets down and then begin with a story, joke, shocking comment, or other attention grabbers. After all, before one can listen, he must hear what is being said. And before he can hear, he must focus attention on the speaker or "tune him in." For instance, a teacher returning materials to other teachers at a faculty meeting was calling out the name on each folder, but was not being heard by his fellow teachers, who were busy chatting with their neighbors. He finally stopped and just held up the material—and suddenly the room quieted down. Each teacher realized that if he wanted his material, he would have to pay attention; no one was going to call his name.

Often teachers will simply say, "Let's have less noise so that we can begin our work," and will then begin giving directions without knowing whether all are paying attention. These exhortations just add to the noise level, which makes the teacher's voice rise and in turn causes the class noise to rise even higher.

The following are four ways to gain the attention of your students.

a) Change the level of noise dramatically, so that everyone will stop to find out what is happening. For instance, try the magic of silence; if you just stand and look around, there will always be some children who will "shush" the others. Use a low voice to set the tone and then begin your lesson.

b) Try to dramatize. The material may be known to you, but it might be an exciting new experience for your group if you present it dramatically—especially in the introductory phase of your lesson. Those who think the attention span of five- or six-year-olds is only fifteen minutes need to be reminded that youngsters can sit and look at TV for hours. Although education may be far different from entertainment, it can learn from it—as "Sesame Street" has proved. The program uses novel ideas to present basic academic skills such as the alphabet.

c) Try a joke to introduce a concept.

d) Inject a mistake while you are reviewing a particular concept, and see if the students can detect it.

(3) Do you have a poor sense of timing?

Successful comedians and actors usually have good timing. It is a skill of audience awareness: they time their material to the capacity of the people. They know when to change their pace, when to shift material, and when to stop.

A teacher who is not sensitive to his audience is in danger of losing it. Consider Mr. Gower, who had planned a math lesson in which he hoped to introduce the base 5 number system. He had planned to devote a thirty-minute period to the lesson and to use the chalk board to give graphic examples of how numbers in base 10 become entirely different in base 5. Most of his presentation involved lecturing and writing on the chalk board. After ten minutes of it, most of his class were not paying attention, and Mr. Gower was annoyed with their seeming lack of ability to listen.

Try the following ideas:

a) Diagnose your presentation. Did you lecture too long without giving students a chance to participate? Become alert to signs of restlessness and inattentiveness and try to find possible causes in your presentation. You might have to use shorter periods with your particular group.

b) Diagnose your material. Does it suit the needs of all your students? No matter what the age level, some children need more concrete or manipulative material at the beginning before they can go on to abstract presentations.

Students always let a teacher know when they are not listening by their restlessness, note passing, or whispering. Be aware of this before the overt signs appear. This will give you time to shift your pace even before they know they have stopped listening.

(4) Do you work with smaller groups of students rather than with the whole class?

Grouping students throughout the grades—upper as well as lower—helps you follow the most important rule of pedagogy: You can teach a child at the level at which he is comfortable. A student who feels inadequate in a subject area will tune you out and stop listening because you are teaching above his ability to comprehend. With small groups you can also more readily notice the problems of individuals and plan ways to strengthen them in the needed areas. Finally, in working with fewer students, you are available to them if they need guidance in a particular area.

What should the other students be doing while you are working with a small group? The next section, "Grouping for Learning," suggests some possibilities.

GROUPING FOR LEARNING

The average elementary-school classroom has three groups working in reading. Miss Scott's second-grade class is typical: one group works with her in a teacher-directed lesson, the second works in a workbook or does some teacher-prepared follow-up activity, the third group is at the other end of the room engaged in independent activity.

Upon entering the room one finds the noise level quite high. Some of the children in the first group, in the reading circle with Miss Scott, appear restless and inattentive; they have finished reading the assigned story and are waiting for the others to finish—and have begun talking to each other. The children in the second group, working in their workbooks, also have some problems. Some are having trouble with a word, others do not quite understand the directions the teacher gave and do not know how to complete their assignments, and still others have rapidly completed their work (and not always correctly) and are now disturbing the rest of the class with loud talking. The third group, engaged in independent activity, has some children who are not interested in the books or games available. They gather around the children still playing and begin to socialize.

By this time Miss Scott can hardly hear any answers or any reading done by the children working with her, and so she adds to the noise: "Shh! I can't hear these children. Stop talking this instant!" Silence reigns for one minute.

The trouble with this class is lack of student involvement; too few children are absorbed in what they are doing. Clues are the restlessness within the reading group and the socialization within the nondirected group. To say that Miss Scott has poor classroom control is a superficial remark, for superimposed control without a foundation of active participation is very rarely effective. Only when students are interested and involved in what they are doing will they adhere to rules and standards. It appears, therefore, that there is a need for differentiated grouping in Miss Scott's classroom.

(1) Are you aware of the different types of grouping?

To insure the interest and involvement of all the students, the teacher must have an in-depth knowledge of varied groupings that can be used at any given time. Some methods of grouping students are used as prescriptions for diagnosed needs. Others are organized to permit children to extend previously learned concepts and to make discoveries on their own.

The following types of grouping are discussed below:
1. ability grouping
2. need grouping
3. interest grouping
4. pupil-team learning
5. learning centers
6. interest centers
7. research grouping

ABILITY GROUPING

This grouping is the most prevalently used. It is based on the idea that a group of children with seeming similarity of ability (homogeneous group) will be able to achieve objectives more effectively than a group of slow and fast learners (heterogeneous group). However, research does not corroborate this belief. As Eash (1966, p. 90) states:

Ability grouping in itself does not produce improved achievement in children. Improved achievement seems rather to result from the manipulation of other complex factors: curriculum adaptation, teaching methods, materials, ability of the teacher to relate to children, and other subtle variables.

Another factor operating against ability grouping is that some students do not fit into any group: they are too slow for one or ahead of others.

Finally, ability grouping could mean a broad range of capabilities within which one might find a variety of needs. Miss Scott had organized her class into three ability groups. But members of the reading group working with her seemed to differ quite markedly in reading speed: some children seemed to need training in phrase reading; others read rapidly but could not answer questions on what they read, indicating the need for intensive work in comprehension skills. This variance in abilities leads us to another type of grouping.

NEED GROUPING

Need groups may be organized as a subgroup within the ability grouping or made up of members of other groups who might benefit from a particular skill lesson. Teaching a whole group a skill that only a few students need will make uninterested students bored and disturbance-prone. Miss Scott's reading group had too many uninterested students who might have profited from need grouping; others could have been given some assignment that would have captured their imagination.

INTEREST GROUPING

Not all students share the same interest in reading materials. Stanchfield (1969) found that one reason why more boys than girls were poorer readers in the primary grades was that the subject matter in their readers did not have a high interest value for them. To avoid this problem, place in the classroom library varied categories of stories and then group the children according to the category that interests them most. There are many easy-to-read publications about cars, space, science, sports, and adventure. Interest grouping can be an independent activity or a subgrouping in an ability group while you are taking care of a need subgroup. Why not spend a day of reading, using only heterogeneous interest grouping? The slower readers would be exposed to intellectual stimulation of a brighter group plus the enjoyment of sharing a mutuality of interest.

PUPIL TEAM-LEARNING

Team-learning is often used without teachers being aware it is a grouping—for example, when children play a word-bingo game, where the leader usually helps them with word recognition. Pupil team-learning also occurs when a group of, say, four children work on color words: one child holds up a card with the word "red" on it; on the back of the card is a square of red paper, so that if the child does not recognize the word "red" he can turn the card around to see the color. This way of providing immediate answers for those who do not know the word can be used for drill work and for reinforcing words previously taught. A group working with self-checking materials is a pupil-team approach. Each child has a turn to play the role of teacher. This type of activity can also be done with math flash cards, the example given on one side and the answer written on the back.

The children working in their workbooks or with teacher-prepared follow-up materials could be working in teams, with the partners helping each other, grading their own papers, then checking their answers against a teacher-prepared answer sheet. If they have incorrect answers, they can correct them immediately. It is important that a beginning teacher understand that if children have finished their work, they will rarely just sit and wait quietly until the teacher invites them to the directed reading circle. They should be preassigned to different areas such as learning centers or interest centers after they have completed their work. If students in Miss Scott's second group working in their workbooks were trained to help each other check their work and then go to a prearranged center, there would be less agitation and noise in that group.

Another type of pupil team-learning is pupil tutoring. One child listens to another one read. Before a tutor is given a job he must be well trained in the procedure. If the tutor knows what he is doing and how to do it, he will enjoy working with another child. When a reader misses a word the tutor tells him the word and writes it on a cumulative word list until five words have been missed. Then reading stops and word study begins. If a child does not remember a word that his tutor gave, he copies it onto a flash card. After a quick drill the tutor can have the child read only the sentences in which the word is found. A tutor can be trained in giving context clues and beginning sound cues. Of course, if a child misses three or four words on a page, he is reading in a book that is too difficult for him. The teacher can check the list for possible word-attack skills needed by the child.

For spelling drill, teamwork is very rewarding if two people play the role of teacher. At first, one calls out a spelling word and the other child writes it on a small chalk board. If it is correct, the child erases the word and passes the chalk board to his partner, who then writes the word called out by him. If a spelling is incorrect, the word is transferred to a list of words that need more drill work. A list such as this can show the teacher that a child might benefit from a linguistic approach to some spelling words. For example, if a child misses words that have similar endings, perhaps a drill in spelling rhyming words might help.

Pupil team-teaching, or tutoring, can be highly rewarding to those children who are not the top group readers. It is satisfying to some children to help others, especially students in the upper grades who are themselves in the low reading groups. As tutors in the primary grades, they also help themselves.

(2) Do you use learning centers and interest centers?

The main difference between learning centers and interest centers is in the purpose for which they are used, since ideas used for one may sometimes be used for the other. A learning center is an activity with a set of directions for students who need additional drill or reinforcement in a given skill. Children are assigned to these centers. An interest center, on the other hand, is a place in which children are free to choose an activity and work on it individually or with a friend. The only rule necessary here is to decide how many can work together at one time.

To assign your students quickly and efficiently to learning centers, make a list of the students on a chart like the one shown below, with five columns for the days of the school week. Suppose you have three learning centers of phonics because these students are members of a special need group. Number your learning centers and arrange to have students go to the learning centers that have been scheduled for them on that particular day. Two days can be assigned as free choice days. If the need is great, you might have five skill centers. You can juggle the number of listening centers according to the number of children that have to be accommodated. Some centers may have as many as eight children, others only two.

		Mon.	Tues.	Wed.	Thurs.	Fri.
1.	John	1	2	3	4	5
2.	Mary	2	3	4	5	1
3.	Jack	3	4	5	1	2
4.	Helen	4	5	1	2	3
5.	Susan	5	1	2	3	4

An alternative chart is the example below. On the left-hand side are slots in which you can insert the names of children. On the right-hand side, at the top and the bottom, are two additional slots into which you can insert a long strip of adding-machine roll paper. Each day the paper is moved so that the children are assigned to their varied learning centers.

Moveable paper

Names			Centers
Mary	Kristine	Barbara	1
John	Tammie	Morris	2
Michael	Suzy	May	3
Joanne	Robert	Jane	4
Kevin	Joy	Richard	5

Nine types of learning centers that may help your students reinforce and possibly extend fundamental skills are discussed on the next page. Some of these ideas might be used as a starting point until you can make up materials for your own group.

1. PHONICS CENTER

While phonics can be used in all the other centers, you may also have a
particular center in which several children can use specific phonic picture
cards and help each other with beginning or final consonants. Or they can
have cards with pictures of the words that have varied vowel sounds in them.

2. LISTENING CENTER

a) You can tape stories and direct children to listen for initial and final
   consonants, diagraphs, blends, and so on, whichever skill is needed. This
   activity can range in complexity from making a mark every time the sound
   is heard to writing the word, depending on the grade level.

b) For rhyming words you can have a work sheet ready with a row of rhyming
   words and the children can be directed to cross out the word that does not
   belong. An answer sheet should be made available for self-checking or else
   you can give the answers after they have finished their work. If children
   are too young to read rhyming words, you can use a rhyming-word tape
   for auditory perception. They can be directed to shut off the tape when
   the listening part is over and click the on button when they are ready to
   correct their own paper or each other's paper.

c) Print a child's name on a strip of paper and place the paper at the top of a
   piece of cardboard on which you have pasted small library-card envelopes.
   Have the child put individual letters in each envelope to match the letters
   in his name.

3. COMPREHENSION AND LISTENING FOR INFORMATION CENTER

a) Have a tape of some riddles available. The children can write or draw
   pictures of the answers. After each riddle there should be a long enough
   pause on the tape so that the children can complete their answers. If they
   are drawing the answer, have them turn off the tape recorder after each
   riddle.

b) Read a story and have children answer questions about the story. Have
   books and check sheets available so they can look up answers.

c) Record on a tape words of more than one syllable and prepare a paper with
   a list of words. As students listen to the words, they can then divide the
   words into syllables on the paper and mark the accented syllables. There
   can also be a space for them to write the syllables. On the tape you can
   immediately give them the right answer after a few minutes of silence; this
   is immediate reinforcement.

d) The syllabication skill can be reinforced with another activity. The student
   listens to a story on tape, reads a chart with scrambled sentences from the
   story, and then writes them correctly in the order in which they happened.
   Again, you should have an answer sheet available for immediate

verification. Another way, for primary-grade children, is to ditto copies of scrambled sentences for the children to cut and paste into a prepared booklet, one sentence to a page, which can then be illustrated.

4. CUT AND PASTE CENTER

a) To learn phonics, children can cut out pictures of things that begin with a given letter, using these to make an alphabet book to take home. Save your Christmas catalogues, magazines, or colorful advertising brochures.
b) Have children cut out letters of the alphabet and paste them on a sheet of paper.
c) To learn classification, children can be told how to locate pictures about a particular subject—for instance, machines, animals, city objects, news about a particular public figure—and may make a scrapbook. Older students may make such scrapbooks from newspaper or magazine articles.
d) To learn classification in grammar, children can cut up a dittoed worksheet that has common nouns, proper nouns, verbs, adjectives, or noun phrases, and paste them under the heading to which they belong. This might surprise some people who think older elementary school children are not interested in cutting and pasting. They enjoy this activity very much.

5. DICTIONARY SKILLS CENTER

a) Younger children can make classifications of zoo or farm animals, food, clothing, family members, and toys. They can look through a picture dictionary and write the words of all zoo animals (or whatever category they have been assigned) they find going from A to Z and give their book a title.
b) The picture dictionary can also be used to find words that begin or end with a consonant, blend, or diagraph and then to make a list of the words. The children can all read the words because the pictures make them self-explanatory.
c) Upper-grade students can locate synonyms for a specified word and write a sentence using the synonyms.
d) Students can alphabetize a given list of words by the first three letters.
e) Ask your pupils to locate the addresses and phone numbers of a given number of names from the telephone directory.

6. LIBRARY SKILLS CENTER

a) Primary-grade children can write a book report, giving the book's title, briefly stating what the book was about and drawing a picture about the part they liked best.
b) Give the children the titles or authors of ten books to alphabetize.

c) For classification, have pupils locate categories of words such as "action words" (verbs) or "name words" (nouns).

d) To improve their comprehension—that is, their understanding of "what," "where," and "when" questions—have students find words or phrases that tell them what happened and where, write them on slips of paper, and put them in the proper columns of a "pocket chart" labeled "what," "where," and "when."

e) To teach children how to locate information, give them a worksheet on which is written several story titles. Have them locate the page number for each story in a book's table of contents and write it next to the title of that story on the worksheet. Markers (pieces of cardboard which help a child focus his eyes on a line of print) may be put under each story title so that children will not confuse the page number on the line below with the correct one.

f) Upper-grade students may write a summary of a story and the reasons to recommend or not recommend it to others.

g) Students can create a dust jacket for a book that will give the main idea of the story in such a way that people will want to buy it.

h) Children can describe the ending of a book, then make up a different ending.

i) Each character in a book can be described, then a story written with the same characters but with a different plot.

7. WRITING CENTER

a) Show students a picture of people in conversation and ask them to write what the people are saying. The use of comic cartoons without conversation might be a good way to begin the activity. Later more sophisticated pictures may be used.

b) Type the beginning of a story on a card and ask the students to write the end of it.

c) For a sequence exercise, use envelopes containing words that make up sentences. Have the children put the words into correct sentence order and write them on paper. Use sentences out of whatever current story they are reading. After the children are experienced in this exercise, they may work with several sentences and put them in sequential order. Code the back of word cards so that they can be returned to their proper envelope after use.

d) Word boxes—boxes with alphabetical dividers in them—can be catalogued according to subject matter such as space words, fairy-tale words, or adventure words, and students can then use them in creative writing.

e) Prepare a folder with a picture in it, under which are words relating to it. Have the student use the words to compose a story about the picture.

f) Same as above, but provide some words that do not go with the picture. Have the student first eliminate the incorrect words.

g) Use a covered box with an opening at the top through which the child may put his hands in order to feel the object inside the box. Have him describe what he feels and then write what he thinks the object is.

h) Have students read an article from a newspaper, then ask them to pretend they are television reporters and must condense the article into two or three sentences for the six-o'clock news report.

i) Tell students how to write minibiographical stories about themselves. Delimit which period or phase of life should be covered—for example, preschool life, early experiences of school life, or hobbies. These stories can later be used as an entire group experience. Leaving out all names, you can read the stories aloud and ask students to guess who wrote them. Here too you can provide a word box with possibly needed vocabulary available for the writers.

j) You can use a book jacket for creative story motivation. The students can write a story that will fit inside the book jacket.

k) Have a box of titles available. A student can pick a title at random and write a story to go with that title.

8. READING IN CONTENT AREAS CENTER

a) For learning about classification and location of information, pupils can be directed to read a plant book, then make a list of the plants and the number of the pages where they are mentioned.

b) For rhyming words, students can use a music book to find the rhyming words in a particular song.

c) Health books can be used for locating information of the kinds of food one should have for breakfast, lunch, or dinner.

d) To teach students how to locate information, give them a category of some sort (such as machines, tools, professions, or trades), then tell them which pages to read and have them find words that belong under each category.

e) Another important skill to reinforce is how to find the main idea. Have each child write a sentence or a paragraph about each page and compare answers with his neighbors. They will find it interesting to note the differences among the opinions held by others.

9. MATH CENTER

a) Using paper cups with numerals written on them and a large supply of buttons, or pinto or lima beans, direct the child to put the number of things into the cup according to the numeral written on it.

b) Buy an inexpensive follow-the-dots booklet and put it in a folder covered with acetate. The children will thus be able to use the same paper over and over again.

c) Have children play tic-tac-toe or draw a picture by plotting given coordinate numbers on graph paper.

d) Have children paste from one to ten pinto beans on ten wooden spatulas, which then become ten-sticks. Children in primary grades need a great deal of counting experiences and this one has a high interest level. When a bean drops off, the stick goes into a stick hopsital (a container) for repair later.

e) Have students use newspaper ads to order supplies for a party or a family dinner; this is a practical and interesting activity for the upper-grade student.

f) Give the students a specified family income and ask them to work out a budget they would enjoy.

g) Provide balance scales with different kinds of materials so that students can figure out how many of one object is equal in weight to how many of another. This activity has high interest value to children of all ages and can be made very simple or sophisticated, depending on the type of questions asked.

INTEREST CENTERS

Whereas children are given directions in the learning centers, they may use interest centers freely and voluntarily, reading books here only because they want to read them. The materials in these centers are used to keep students occupied and involved when they have completed their other work and are waiting for others to finish.

Discuss rules and regulations with students before the interest centers are set up.

a) Introduce each game before it is put at their disposal.

b) Make sure they understand what to do and how to take care of the games, establishing this at the outset. Check daily to see whether games have been put away. Occasional reinforcement of the rules will firmly establish good housekeeping details. In this way your materials will last longer and give more service to those using them.

c) Store all materials close to where they will be used so that students do not have to walk to the other end of the room to get them.

Some games that may be used at interest centers are as follows:

a) Commercial word and math games.

b) Crossword puzzles.

c) Jigsaw puzzles. (Put a mark on the underside so that you can recognize which puzzle each piece belongs to.

d) Use felt shapes on felt boards for creating interesting and colorful designs that can be transferred to paper.

e) Teacher-made games like "Concentration" for words, shapes, or arithmetical operations.

Limit the number of games you make available and change them often so the students do not tire of them. Put them back for use after they have been off the game shelf for a few weeks.

The learning center is used to give additional practice needed in the reinforcement of a previously learned skill. The interest center is used for transitional periods when children have completed their assignments and want to relax with games. Interest centers can also be used as the stage setting for enrichment learning. These differences should be carefully considered when you are organizing your materials.

RESEARCH GROUPING

For science and social studies reports and special projects, it helps to form a group of children with heterogeneous abilities. The slower readers can find pictures and discuss them or help organize a scrapbook. They will be sparked by the more capable students and will enjoy working with them.

The more able students can work on collecting information from newspapers and the encyclopaedia. Preparing the presentation of such a report involves the group in how best to present it. The most important learning is that of working with other people and experiencing the interaction of ideas and responsibilities.

(3) Are you flexible in using these varied groups?

It is important to keep in mind the best use of a particular grouping and when to use it; however, you should also try not to jump around indiscriminately. Start with achievement grouping, since it is the easiest to form. In each student's cumulative record you will often find the name of his previous reader, along with comments about his performance.

As these groups work with you, note their special problems and interests. You can usually determine this information from classroom performance rather than from written records. You get to know which children enjoy responsibilities and duties and which children do not enjoy working with others, regardless of how proficient they are. You could use pupil team-learning within an ability grouping when you are working with a small special-needs group.

Members of a special-interest group can begin their work after they have completed some workbook assignment. Others can be doing some of their research assignment. This intricate programming can be efficiently handled if the children are carefully prepared and all assignments are noted on a large program schedule.

All these classroom activities require intensive organization. Each child should know that there is a written master program for students where he can check his schedule to determine exactly what he is to do. At first the planning takes a great deal of time, but the more children are involved in this type of program the more proficient they become in working as a member of one team or another. For the teacher there is gratification in seeing students actively and cooperatively involved in learning together.

WORKING EFFECTIVELY WITH CHILDREN
OF VARIED ABILITIES

This problem faces most teachers, but beginning teachers have more difficulty solving it—namely, the problem of coping with the various levels of abilities encountered in the classroom. This problem can be expressed as several questions.

(1) Are you using your teaching time most effectively?

Miss Jenkins, while teaching her class the basics of division, discovered that Peter had not quite mastered the operation of subtraction. Since it is a vital part of division, she thought it would be best to help him over that stumbling block right then and there. Before she knew it, it was time for recess and the children who had been ready to move on into the new operation were not able to do so. Miss Jenkins believed that she had helped Peter. Perhaps she did, but in the interim she lost the interest of the majority of her group.

There is a tendency for some beginning teachers to be drawn into spending a major portion of their teaching time with children who are slow learners. Be aware that there is a loss of valuable learning time for those who are proficient enough to proceed to a new learning experience. Since children do not take kindly to boredom, they become restless and inattentive, and this condition sets the stage for behavior problems.

To avoid individuals becoming spectators to Peter's learning problem become aware of the weaknesses and strengths of your students. Before you teach a new concept, analyze what prerequisites are needed to master it. Miss Jenkins, for instance, could have tested her students in the previously taught operations, thus avoiding the common teachers' pitfall of assuming that all their children understand what they have been taught previously.

If Peter were not the only one needing assistance, Miss Jenkins could organize a special-needs group of students who could be helped in this operation before going on with learning a new one. The rest of her group could be working in a workbook, solving operational problems they already knew, or working at math interest centers with math games that reinforce their skills. For math geniuses, she could use the enrichment math books available and the puzzlers found in commercial math games booklets.

If Peter were the only one with the problem, he might need outside professional tutoring, or a few private sessons with Miss Jenkins or a student tutor to help him catch up. Such tutoring should be on a one-to-one basis so that Peter will be spared any embarrassment. Pre-testing would have helped Miss Jenkins diagnose his problem so that she could plan her teaching time most efficiently.

Apportion your time so that no one student or group takes up most of your time. The faster learner can usually do more work on his own, but his program demands intensive planning and organization. He needs materials that will keep him moving along at an interesting and stimulating pace. He also needs encouragement and attention from you, sometimes more than the slow learner because his standards are usually high and he demands more from himself.

Grouping plans for your class will aid you in using your time most effectively. No matter how homogeneous you think your class is, you are sure to find different ranges of ability—especially in the upper-elementary grades. Use the ideas of varied groupings discussed earlier to reach and challenge all your students.

(2) Do you use the type of motivation suited to the ability level of your students?

For the fast learner one can use the type of challenging motivation that might excite him into action. However, for the slow learner, that same exciting idea may cause him to back away, especially if he has experienced failure in many areas of his school career. School life for such a student is often a precarious path of "failure avoidance." Because any new idea might lead to failure, he is not comfortable with any unfamiliar learning situation.

Mr. Halder brought an extra table into his room on which he put junk objects such as rusty nails, old buttons, balloons, wooden wheels, rocks, a water basin, boxes of different kinds of soil, and the like. Around these objects he placed various sizes of magnets, magnifying glasses, and a small balance scale. He had his students circulate around the table and watched their response. The tremendous interest of his students was revealed by the rapid series of questions this display evoked from them. At the height of their curiosity as to the purpose of the table and its contents, Mr. Halder put up a sign that read, "Can you plan an experiment?" He soon noted a difference in the reaction of his slower students. At a later time, Mr. Halder questioned some of the children who did not spend time working at this table. Their answers indicated they did not know where to begin; the challenge of choosing, planning, and setting up an experiment acted as a deterrent. They seemed to need more direction, a more specific approach, with small-step instructions of what to do. They enjoyed working with the unstructured display, but as soon as a challenge was added they lost interest. Certain students, in other words, needed motivation of a different kind.

Remember that the slower learner needs "failure-proof" experiences that will build success upon success and give him constant encouragement. The faster learner needs less repetition, more meaningful independent explorations, and challenging activities.

(3) Do you vary your materials for your slow learners?

The basic rule of teaching young children is to introduce a concept by presenting it with concrete examples. From this point you can begin to move from the concrete to the abstract. The primary-grade teacher is usually well stocked with concrete teaching aids. When teaching shapes, for instance, he need not draw a picture of a square and tell the children the name of it; rather he can introduce the idea using boxes of squares and pieces of square-shaped material that the pupils can manipulate. The students can then be asked to find things shaped like a square in their environment, reproduce the shape on paper, and find squares in a row of varied shapes. Similarly, a child can be taught to count objects before being exposed to the numeral. He then sees the numeral with the number of things that it is used for. The numeral will not be used alone until he understands the fiveness of the numeral "5."

No matter what the grade level, the slower learner must have many concrete experiences before he is exposed to an abstract concept. Manipulative materials will involve him and help him learn better—and can also free the teacher to work with the faster learners. Manipulative aids are especially helpful when coupled with tape recorders with tapes telling students what to do with the aids. Small flannel boards and flannel cutouts, for example, can give children drill work in introductory multiplication: they can form two sets of three objects, three sets of three objects, and so on, and as they are forming these sets they can be told the multiplication table to which these sets belong. A follow-up activity is to have students draw the sets and then write the abstraction it represents, such as $2 \times 3 = 6$. The use of concrete objects helps them conceptualize what multiplication means, and repetitive drill work—if done in meaningful and interesting ways—helps them arrive at an understanding of a concept.

If you do not have ear phones for your listening center, do not let that keep you from using a tape recorder. You can put a group of children at the other end of your room and group them around the tape recorder. Modulate the volume so that they can hear what is said. Usually the sound on the tape will not disturb you, for it will be your own voice.

The tape recorder can also be used with your other students while you are working with the slow learners. For example, you can be giving a spelling pretest through the tape recorder. At the end of the test you can give the answers by slowly spelling out the words. The students can then study and practice the words they have missed. Thus, with these techniques you can be in two places at once and reach fast and slow learners simultaneously.

Another good teaching aid is the individual slate. Children enjoy writing on slates with chalk and then erasing what they have written. When you are working with a group, have all the children write an answer on their slates and hold them up for you to see so that you can note and correct mistakes right then. Everyone should be called upon to answer and no one neglected. This aid has been used not only in primary grades but also in upper grades, especially with slower learners.

The individual slate is a very inexpensive and easily made teaching tool. The heavy gray cardboard sometimes called chip board is on requisition in most schools. One can find varied sizes ready cut. Buy a green chalk board paint and cover the chip board. When the board is completely dry, rub some chalk over the entire surface, erase it, and the individual chalk boards will be primed and ready for use.

(4) Have you considered a modified individualized learning program for your fast learners?

If there is a very wide range of abilities in your class and a group of children who far outdistance the rest, they should be permitted to move ahead at their own pace. This type of program, to be effective, must be supervised by the teacher with regular conferences.

Give the student a choice of books he may read on his own, taking care that his choice is one he can read comfortably without missing more than one or two words on a page. When he does miss a word, have him write it in his notebook. At conference time you can check his word list to see if he needs a skill lesson in a special-needs group that will aid him with that word when he meets it again.

Each child on the individualized reading program can keep a diary of his progress in terms of stories or books read, prepare book reviews that he can share with other students, or be sent to a learning center to reinforce a needed skill. In this way the fast learner need not be held back but can embark on an individualized reading program. He may become part of the directed reading lesson when a particular skill is being taught, but otherwise he can read at his own pace and not have to wait for the rest of the group to catch up. Conferences can be held during a reading group's silent reading time or during a work period when you are free to move from child to child and give help when needed. The modified individualized learning plan can be used in all other subject matter. In mathematics, enrichment materials in supplementary textbooks will help the fast learner work at his own pace; he can be brought back to a particular group whenever he needs a particular skill lesson. (For a good source book on a fully individualized program see Stahl and Anzalone, 1970.)

To reach fast and slow learners and challenge both requires creative, knowledgeable programming with a flexibility governed by the level of your students rather than the demands of your program.

DEVELOPING INTERESTING LESSONS

Will all your students find a specific lesson interesting? Probably not. Children have different interests and tastes.

Still, there are four tendencies present in most children. First, they enjoy being the center of interest. Second, they are apt to find any subject matter interesting if they feel successful in that area. Third, if a lesson is on a topic they have a special interest in because of a hobby or favorite sport, they will find that lesson also interesting. Finally, most students will find lessons that include a new world of ideas or a new way of doing things interesting because novelty adds a spark of excitement.

(1) Are you interested in what you are doing?

In the book of Ecclesiastes it is written that there is nothing new under the sun. But ideas sometimes look new after your mind has refreshed them or organized them differently. A preacher, asked where he got his wonderful ideas, replied that ideas were like pearls: he could not manufacture them, but he could string them together in an interesting way. Teachers can develop the same skill; using something they hear or see, they can make it their own by presenting it in a slightly different way. This constant search for new ideas will keep the teacher interested and enthusiastic about new approaches that can be discovered, and this enthusiasm will be transmitted to the students.

Not all the new approaches will work with all students, but some of them will help to avoid the deadening effect of dull drill and repetition, which causes some children to change from eager kindergarten scholars to disillusioned, frustrated school-haters. Hopefully the enthusiasm of those who do respond to novel ideas will attract the interest of the others. Enthusiasm is contagious, and students do get caught up in the excitement that novel ideas create.

(2) Have you used the egocentricity of the child as motivation?

Language experience stories are absorbing reading for each individual author because the story is about himself and a world he is familiar with. The child writes a story about an interesting experience he has had or an autobiographical sketch. If he cannot do his own writing, he can dictate the story to you. This story will become his reader from which you will be able to choose his words for use in a skill lesson. Lee and Allen (1963) state that what a child can say he can write, and what he writes he can read. In essence, this method revolves about the individual.

A slow learner in one subject might not be slow in another. Thus, a good math student who is having difficulty with reading could be exposed to the language experience method. The stories he writes become his reading material. In primary grades the teacher can type the student's dictation; in upper grades the student can write his own material. The important step is the motivational one, since it is a personal experience or feeling. The student reads what he has dictated or written, after the teacher corrects his grammar and idiomatic expressions.

In a second-grade class, Henry was shown a picture of an angry little girl. When asked to tell a story about the picture he said, "Her is mad." The teacher said, "Yes, she is mad, isn't she?" and then wrote the corrected grammatical form. However, Henry read the grammatical form that he had dictated. The behavioral objective in this lesson is to help Henry read a sentence he has dictated. It is not to teach him grammar. It is important to remember that he will read only what he says.

Use of the language experience approach to reading as an additional teaching technique, along with basal readers and supplementary books, will help children feel successful in an area where they usually feel inadequate.

Some of the motivational ideas that can be used to elicit language experience stories are as follows:

a) Reactions to an emotionally charged picture.
b) Reactions to mood music.
c) Solutions to complete unresolved plots in a story on film.
d) Descriptions of exciting holidays.
e) Descriptions of the students' families.
f) Descriptions of what students would like to do in school.
g) Autobiographies or recollections of what students remember from their past experiences.
h) Descriptions of hopes and expectations of their future.
i) Descriptions of what it might feel like to be an inanimate object.

The varieties are as endless as the teacher and students' imaginations, and they are a delightful way to vary a reading program and make the reading lesson interesting and absorbing.

In primary grades many teachers write labels for classroom articles and attach them to desks, chairs, closets, and the like. You can also have the child draw a picture of himself and label the parts of his body, making a chart available so that each writer can work independently. This interesting project can have a good deal of incidental learning. Eventually, you might remove the chart to check whether the children can write words such as face, mouth, hair, and ears.

No matter what the grade level, students find it exciting to measure their heights and discover who is the tallest or shortest person in the class. The teacher can graph the height of all the people in the room. It is also interesting for each student to keep a diary of the fluctuations of his weight when he weighs himself at different times of the day—an activity that reinforces the operations of addition and subtraction. Older students can investigate the correlation between height and weight and can work out problems of finding the average weight of all the pupils in class and seeing who comes closest to it. These are supplementary lessons for fun, drill, and reinforcement at the same time.

The use of problems such as dividing marbles among friends, preparing for a party and planning for different quantities of supplies for a specific number of guests, are problems children might find absorbing. Use a folder with a Sears catalog and order form in it, tell your students they have $100 to spend as they wish, and have them write out their order, calculate and record the price of the gifts they want, and total the cost. This assignment contains many math operations as well as reading and writing skills. Once you think of lesson planning in this way, you will discover many more ideas that had not occurred to you before.

(3) Are you arranging your lessons so that all children feel successful?

This worthy goal is one of the most difficult to attain—especially when the only grouping in a class is ability grouping. When all the children are expected to be able to handle an assignment, students with lesser ability become bored because they feel inadequate. If they do not understand or if they cannot read, then no matter how novel or interesting the subject, they will drop out and lose precious learning time. On the other hand, a feeling of doing something that they know is right is absorbing to them because they feel successful. When teaching in an inner-city school, one of the authors noted that children always enjoyed copying stories from a reading book. Even if they could not read all the words it somehow pleased them to write the story. There were no behavior problems when they were occupied this way. They knew that whatever they were writing was correct because the words were in a book; thus, they felt successful in writing the story.

Fader and McNeil (1966), writing of their experiences teaching teen-aged boys in a reform school, tell of trying to raise the students' reading ability, which ranged from second- to fourth-grade level. One of their most important rules was that no hard-cover books were allowed in the schoolroom, since the boys had known only failure with these types of books; instead, there were paperback books, magazines, and newspapers. The only obligation the students had to fulfill was to write a minimum of one page a day. This was a failure-proof assignment because they had the choice of writing about anything they were interested in, or if they could not write on their own they were free to copy any of the materials they had in the room. This choice gave them a way to feel successful with the written word and started them on a phenomenally successful learning experience. In just a few months time there was a gain of several years in their reading ability. Success feeds on success and once children feel the buoyant feeling of doing well, many of them begin to soar.

When students are having difficulty in some subject matter, investigate to discover the level at which they feel successful. Each successful experience is a positive reinforcement to learn even more, and this feeling of success makes everything they do very interesting.

(4) Are you using special-interest groupings or enthusiasm about hobbies to stimulate interest in lessons?

Children are natural collectors. A table display of what your class is collecting can be used as a starting point for science lessons, language experience stories for reading, and creative math problems. For example, one second-grade class had several children who collected dinosaur models. Each child brought his collection to school. The teacher asked them to initial each piece so that the exhibitors were sure to get back their own models. A bar-graph chart was made showing how many dinosaurs each child had brought. Everyone became enthused about the display and began bringing in books about dinosaurs. The school library added to the research corner. A whole unit was built around these dinosaurs. Committees were established and each committee was given a specific type of dinosaur on which to write a report. Another chart was prepared showing the height of each type of dinosaur. This class had been working on descriptive words and so a chart was prepared entitled "Adjectives for Dinosaurs." A model world of the age of the dinosaurs was created on the display table; this helped other children in making a mural of the varied types of dinosaurs. The interest level was extremely high in the reading, writing, and research involved in this special-interest area. For a culmination, the class organized a television show called "Stump the Experts." Guests were given a list of possible questions they might ask, and each team of experts on a particular dinosaur sat at a panel table and was questioned. They were all fully prepared and ready because of the high interest this topic generated.

You can use car collections, rocks, dolls, shells, or seeds from various plants. This area of special interest is rich in materials from which a teacher can create an exciting world of learning and discovery.

(5) Do you try fresh and novel approaches that create an excitement about learning?

In the methods courses you learn how to teach various subject matter found in the curriculum. These methods are good for the initial exposure, but all learning needs drill work, repetition, and reinforcement. For these you need to enliven the lessons with different approaches to the same goal. For example, many teachers use an eclectic approach. They use basal readers, booklets by children in the language experience approach, supplementary readers, library books, magazines, and all sundry materials that are suitable and of interest to their group.

Another novel idea is for children to make up riddles and then make books of these riddles. This is a new source of reading material and a mind-stretching method at the same time. All ages find these riddles stimulating. For the younger children subjects of riddles must be familiar, everyday articles.

A variation is to paste a picture inside a folder, have a child look at it and give a clue to it (such as "It is a fruit"), then give other children three chances to guess what it is. If they do not get it, the riddle maker can give them another clue (such as "It is small and red"), and this continues until someone guesses it. You can then write down the clues, type them, and put them into the folder, which can then be added to the library collection with the author's name on the cover. A word of caution: If a child gives a clue that is practically a giveaway, use the experience to train children in how to devise clues that tell just enough without giving the subject away. If a youngster gives the clue "Something you eat with" for a spoon, most children will guess it right away. Use such an instance to discuss the type of clues it is best to use initially, such as what it is made of, its shape, and so forth. It is only the final clue that should reveal its function or use.

Why not have your students learn Morse code? A Morse code practice key can be obtained from army surplus stores. You can then chart the code and have regular training sessions during independent activities. Students can send each other secret messages, practice spelling drill, or play the game "Guess My Word." At first they can write down each letter separately. Later, after they become more proficient, they can do it by the word. You can make up sheets of paper that look like this:

Fill in the correct letter:

I. 1. _____   II. 1. _____   III. 1. _____
    2. _____   2. _____   2. _____
    3. _____   3. _____   3. _____
                           4. _____   4. _____
                                                    5. _____

When all letters are filled in, it is a sentence. You can use words that are given in spelling. This method is an enjoyable approach that can be used for reinforcement. If the sound of the key is distracting, use flashing bulbs to simulate the dots and dashes.

If you want to have students practice their handwriting skills, it is far more interesting to accomplish this task in new and different ways such as writing letters to other schools, countries, or classes in the same school. The students can even exchange letters in the classroom while playing an interesting game. For example, each student draws the name of a classmate from a hat, not revealing the name he drew. Each student then writes a letter describing himself to the person whose name he drew. The teacher collects the letters and later delivers them to the addressees without letting them know who sent the letter. The recipient takes his letter and reads it to the group, after which he has two guesses as to who wrote it. After the letter is read and the author is guessed or his identity revealed, the letter reader must grade the penmanship and write a statement of the grade. Many other skills can be practiced in a similarly enjoyable way (Tiedt and Tiedt, 1965).

CASE INCIDENTS

Case incident 1: Poor timing

Betty, a child in Mrs. Harris's sixth-grade class, was not performing at the high level indicated by her test scores. Upon investigating her home environment, Mrs. Harris discovered that Betty's parents did not show any interest in her school activities.

To alleviate this problem Mrs. Harris decided to provide Betty with individual instruction, hoping that such attention would not only improve Betty's math skills but also encourage her to work harder.

During an art period, Mrs. Harris took Betty to a corner of the room and drilled her with flash cards of the multiplication tables.

"Now, Betty, I want to help you improve your 'times table' while the children are doing their art. Give me an answer for every card and we'll review the mistakes made. Math is very important and you can return to art when I see that you are also participating in class math."

Betty was very hesitant in her responses and showed a great deal of resentment. Mrs. Harris tried to be understanding, knowing that Betty *did* know most of the answers but was fearful that an answer might be incorrect. With encouragement, she began to answer willingly, and even gained enough confidence to answer problems more quickly. Mrs. Harris decided to instruct Betty during every art lesson in hopes that her general class participation would also improve. After three weeks, there was some improvement in Betty's math skills but none in her attitude toward the class.

On rejoining the math class, Betty responded to only two out of three problems correctly.

Mrs. Harris became aggravated. "Betty, we went over this drill card only a few minutes ago. You couldn't have forgotten."

"Well, I did forget, and I don't care anyway," Betty replied. "Why do you always pick on me? I don't bother the class anyway."

The other students were now distracted and began to murmur ridicule toward Betty. Mrs. Harris demanded order and determinedly tried to elicit an answer from Betty. But the child became sulky and completely refused to participate in the drill.

Discussion Questions. Why did Mrs. Harris's plan fail? Did she diagnose the problem correctly? What should her next step be? How can a teacher determine what is positive reinforcement to a child? How can a student be given special help without embarrassment?

STUDENT NOTES

Case incident 2: Getting by

Rosa attended the first grade in a large urban area. English was usually spoken at home, but she was exposed to Spanish also, and was thus bilingual. Rosa had not learned to read or write using the Initial Teaching Alphabet system. (The i/t/a system has forty-four symbols instead of the conventional twenty-six; each of the forty-four symbols represents only one sound.) Rosa often watched other children or drew pictures instead of completing her assignments. She was a loner during class, and at recess she watched the other children play, but did not interact with them even when asked.

Let us now look at some of Rosa's classroom behavior. Whenever she was asked an individual question that required an affirmative or negative response, her answer was always "no." If she was asked to reexamine the question or her answer, she would change her answer to "yes." Rosa was in a small group of five members who were all slow readers. On one occasion, after a story had been read orally in class, the teacher asked Rosa a question about the main point of the story. "Did Sally's dog learn a new trick?" The teacher looked her straight in the eye and gave no clue to the correct answer. Rosa seemed totally confused. She shrugged her shoulders and replied, "I don't know."

In a group discussion Rosa was very withdrawn. After the group was asked a question, she waited for the others to answer and then imitated their responses. The teacher once asked Rosa a question she was unable to answer, and another student answered the question correctly. When the teacher repeated the question to her, Rosa said, "I don't remember what he said."

During the creative writing period, the children were encouraged to express their ideas, using the i/t/a method of phonetic spelling. Rosa merely scribbled on her paper and made no attempt to write the sounds she heard. She knew that eventually the teacher would ask her what she wanted to say and would write it for her. All Rosa had to do, then, was copy what the teacher had written, and therefore did not have to use her initiative.

Rosa memorized the first few pages of her reader and "read" it quite willingly. As soon as she reached a page that was not memorized, she was stumped. She stopped reading and made no attempt to use the phonetic sounds for the words. The teacher tried to drill her on her vocabulary with flash cards and found she did not know the words or even the sounds of the letters. Rosa made no attempt to match the word or letter with a sound. She guessed at all the words. Once, pointing to the word "see," the teacher asked, "What letter does this word begin with?"

"S," Rosa replied.

"Very good, Rosa," the teacher said. "Now that we know it begins with an 's,' what is the word?"

"Her," Rosa replied.

Discussion Questions.   What can a teacher do to diagnose learning difficulties such as Rosa's? What instructional techniques should be used to help her? What teaching devices can be used to determine if actual learning has taken place? Would Rosa progress faster with more individual help such as with a tutor, older child, or bilingual classmate? How does being bilingual affect her learning difficulties?

STUDENT NOTES

Case incident 3: Individual attention

Linda, a second-grader, did not appear interested in her work and was slow compared to other children. Instead of doing her work she created disturbances in the back of the room, which was divided into different sections and table clusters. Linda sat on the far side of the room with two very active boys and a quiet and rather capable girl. The following describes a typical day.

During reading period, Mrs. White divided the children into groups according to their reading ability. She worked with the best readers for twenty minutes. Linda, as well as a few other children, could not read and were left to themselves with some other work to do.

Linda began to play with her lunch money.

Mrs. White said, "Linda, put your money down and get to work."

Linda answered, "I don't know what to do."

"Mrs. White left the reading table to see what she could give Linda to do. She handed her an unfinished sheet that she discovered in her work folder and told her to finish it. Linda took the paper, looked at it and at her teacher with blank eyes. "When you finish the paper, Linda, bring it to me so I can check it," said Mrs. White, and then left the table.

After a few minutes, Linda rose from her chair and began to wander around the room, doing nothing. Mrs. White saw her, but said nothing and continued with her work.

Later, the special reading teacher came to work with the students who were below grade level. Linda took one look at her and said, "Oh, no! There she is again. I don't like her!"

In her little circle at the front of the room, Linda sat staring at her teacher with the same blank eyes. Every time the special teacher asked her a question, she stared blankly and said nothing. She did this all through the lesson. After a while, the teacher stopped directing questions to her.

But Linda did like a particular teacher aide and worked well for her. Within a matter of a few days, she was able to complete many of her unfinished papers as long as the aide was near her or watching her closely.

Noticing that Linda was capable of doing her work, the aide told the teacher that all she needed was a little more personal attention. The teacher explained to her that with thirty-five students in the room, it was impossible for her to give that kind of attention to one girl and that Linda would have to try and keep up as best she could, just like the other pupils.

The teacher aide was unable to be in the class for a few days and when she returned, she found almost all of Linda's papers untouched or incomplete. When this was brought to the attention of Mrs. White, she glowered at the paper and said, "Well, that's Linda for you!"

Discussion Questions.   What steps can Mrs. White take to help her identify and diagnose Linda's problem? Would it be better to separate Linda from the rest of the children and put her in a special class? What are the advantages and disadvantages of this approach? How can Mrs. White organize her reading program for individualized instruction?

STUDENT NOTES

Case incident 4: The incipient failure

During a handwriting lesson in which the students were learning to write their names, Tom appeared to be just doodling rather than practicing his name. When approached by the teacher, Mrs. Jones, Tom's first response was, "I can't do it. I can't write my name. It is too hard."

Looking down at his paper, Mrs. Jones remarked, "You don't seem to be trying very hard. I only see your name written twice on your paper."

"I just can't write, Mrs. Jones," said Tom, grinning sheepishly as if he were proud of the fact.

Mrs. Jones took Tom's hand in hers and helped him form the letters of his name. After a few more times, Tom was able to write his name by himself, in clear, well-formed letters, and began practicing along with the rest of the class.

Mrs. Jones made a mental note of Tom's reluctance to try anything on his own. He seemed to have a fear of failure and thus tried to cover up his fear by appearing to be proud of the fact that he could not do something along with the rest of the class.

Later that day, Mrs. Jones's suspicions about Tom were further confirmed as she noticed his actions during the introduction of a new math lesson. After explaining the lesson on the board, Mrs. Jones asked the class if they had any questions. Immediately, a few hands shot up and Mrs. Jones proceeded to answer them, which involved a review of the process she had just explained. Again asking for questions and seeing none, Mrs. Jones assigned a page in the math workbook to supplement the lesson she had just presented. As she walked around the room to observe the students' progress, she noted that all were busily involved in solving the assigned problems except Tom. As she approached him, Mrs. Jones saw that again Tom had made only a few attempts (all incorrect) and was just sitting and fidgetting with his pencil.

"What's wrong, Tom? Don't you understand the assignment?" Mrs. Jones asked.

Tom just shrugged his shoulders and gave a little grin.

"Tom, do you know what problems you're supposed to be doing?"

"Yes," replied Tom, "but I can't do them."

"Well, why didn't you raise your hand when I asked for questions or when I started walking around the room to help people?"

Again Tom shrugged his shoulders and grinned sheepishly.

Since it was apparent he did not understand the lesson, Mrs. Jones sat down with him and took about ten minutes to explain it. After this he had no problem completing the assignment, but yet when the class went over it orally he refused to raise his hand to volunteer an answer. This perplexed Mrs. Jones, since she knew that Tom understood the lesson and had the correct answers. He seemed resigned to the fact that his answers could not possibly be right.

A few days later, Tom again exhibited his defeatist attitude. All of the children had been making dioramas (little scenes in shoeboxes) at home and bringing them in as part of their study of geography. Mrs. Jones noticed that Tom had brought a diorama in and asked him to show her which one on the shelf it was (few had their owners' names). Tom just grinned and said, "No, it's too crummy."

By his mannerisms, it was obvious to Mrs. Jones that Tom really did want her to know which diorama was his—but he wanted to be coaxed a little.

"I'm sure it's a very good one," she persisted. "Which one is it?"

"It's this one," Tom said, "but it's no good."

In all of Tom's work, this defeatist attitude prevailed. No matter what the subject, it seemed that whenever a new lesson was presented, Tom resigned himself to the fact that he could not do it. However, as Mrs. Jones helped him each time, Tom easily understood the concept and could then proceed to finish the lesson on his own. Obviously, Tom was not subnormal in intelligence; in fact, he was high average.

Discussion Questions.   Why did Tom's success in his schoolwork thrive on individual instruction from Mrs. Jones for each new assignment? How could Mrs. Jones motivate Tom to work on his own? What are some possible reasons for Tom's "failure complex?" Based on what you know about Tom, what would his actions most likely be toward his fellow classmates—for instance, at recess in a game situation?

STUDENT NOTES

Case incident 5: Boredom—dead end to learning

Many of the children in Patsy's fourth-grade class were not motivated to work. Some of the children did the work nevertheless, without enthusiasm, but a few refused to do anything, Patsy in particular.

Students were usually given an assignment to work on in class for a number of days. During the whole class period, Patsy either would do absolutely nothing or would doodle in her book, and the teacher did not notice it or simply ignored it. However, when the paper was due, Patsy never had it. An encounter with Patsy and the teacher went something like this:

Teacher: Patsy, what is the answer to number 3?
Patsy: I don't know.
Teacher: Why don't you know?
Patsy: I didn't do the assignment.
Teacher: Why didn't you do the assignment?"
Patsy: I didn't want to.
Teacher: Why didn't you want to?
Patsy: Because I don't like this class and I am not interested in what you are doing.

At that point the teacher was at a loss as to what to do. She had tried many new techniques hoping to motivate the children. Sometimes she had even let the class decide what they would like to do, but most of the children could not even think of an idea except getting out of class. She was at a disadvantage because the school demanded a certain curriculum even though the students were not interested in the subject matter. The teacher might have taught her class any way she liked, but certain material had to be covered. If she let the students decide what to do, they decided to do nothing. Even if she varied her techniques to try to motivate interest in the subject, the students still did not care and still refused to work.

Discussion Questions. Motivation is commonly mentioned by teachers as being a major classroom problem. Diagnose possible causes for lack of motivation in a classroom. Does "schooling" contribute to lack of motivation? In what ways? What relationships exist between motivation and learning? What would you do in the present situation?

STUDENT NOTES

Case incident 6: Off with the old, on with the new

One problem facing many teachers today is the changing curriculum. English is undergoing many changes and the teacher is sometimes at a loss as to exactly what form of English to teach.

One particular seventh-grade class was just beginning to learn the "new" grammar. The children did not grasp the related aspects of the two grammars and the teacher had to present the material so that the children would be able to understand it. Since the class had had grammar throughout school, the school board expected the students to grasp the new material rapidly. When the teacher began teaching the new grammar, she found that the students did not understand what they were doing. Essentially they had to unlearn the old grammar in order to understand the new grammar; with both types the students were thoroughly confused.

The teacher followed the new book rather closely because the children felt more secure, yet the new book did not allow enough practice time. He then allowed a few extra days to go over the material and set numerous examples. Actually, he tried to drill the information into the students because they did not understand the advantages of the new grammar. They were more unwilling to learn because they already had learned one grammar and did not wish to learn another. They did not see the relationships between the two grammars and could not divorce the old grammar while working on the new. Consequently, they had closed their minds because they did not want to let go of what they had learned in exchange for something that did not really give them new information.

Discussion Questions. How can the teacher effectively teach the new grammar (a grammar he may not fully accept himself) to students who are unwilling to exchange what they have already learned for something new? Is it really better for students to change from the old to the new? How can the teacher best make the transition?

STUDENT NOTES

Case incident 7: Keep working!

Mrs. Smith was the teacher of a second-grade class in a middle-income neighborhood. She had been teaching for several years but had been receiving complaints from her students' parents about the amount of work that she had them take home. They were receiving low grades from her also because they did not do their work, did poorly on their tests, and constantly caused problems. The following was a selection of her morning schedule.

8:45—Morning bell rings
9:00—Meet with the Robins (reading group 1)
      a) review from the day before
      b) read new story
      c) discuss new story
      d) give assignments
9:15—Meet with the Bluebirds (reading group 2)
      a) review from the day before
      b) read new story
      c) discuss new story
      d) give assignments
9:30—Meet with the Eagles (reading group 3)
      a) review from the day before
      b) read new story
      c) discuss new story
      d) give assignments
9:40—Recess
9:50—Math

Discipline was a major problem for Mrs. Smith. Her students were constantly getting out of control. She was always yelling at them (it seemed to be the only way to get their attention—and yet even then they would not listen to her). Some students were always causing problems and disrupting the class. Thus, her entire schedule was thrown off. According to Mrs. Smith, however, that really did not matter since the Eagles were her slow group; they would never understand what she was trying to teach them, whether she met with them or not. She kept them occupied with ditto pages to color about the stories that they had read. Most of the time she was able to meet with this group just before recess. They were told to complete their workbook pages at home because there was not enough classroom time.

Mrs. Smith was quite upset with all of the parents complaining about her. She believed that most of her problems were caused by the children and that she was not to blame.

Discussion Questions. What are some of the problems Mrs. Smith might be having? Can instructional problems lead to other problems? In what way? Should second-grade students have work to take home? How could she diagnose her problem? What are some possible plans which might alleviate her problem?

STUDENT NOTES

Case incident 8: Where do they belong?

From 10:10 to 11:00 A.M. every day, Mr. Williams taught mathematics. It was a second-grade class, but two-thirds of the class had trouble mastering even first-grade addition. Because of this extreme difference in ability, Mr. Williams divided the class into three groups according to a test and personal observation. Out of twenty-four students, six were in the top group, twelve in the middle, and six in the low.

Mr. Williams's problem was finding enough time to work with all three groups. The slow group needed the most time; they were still on addition and needed to be boosted to grade level. The fast group was learning about groups of ten and were at grade level, but they could not work independently at their desks. Although they could have helped the slower students with their math problems, it caused too many behavior problems and disturbed Mr. Williams and his work with the large middle group. The middle group could not be combined with either of the other groups because none of them had understood addition by tens and yet had passed the addition stage of the low group and were ready to work on subtraction. They all needed to be brought up to the second-grade level. Since the middle group was so large, it took longer to help them and shortened the hour for the other groups.

Grouping caused many organizational and discipline problems for Mr. Williams.

Discussion Questions. A teacher cannot be at all four corners of the room at the same time. How can a teacher use groups and still maintain his mental health through proper organization? If more time is needed for one subject, how can time from other subjects be utilized? If a teacher has difficulty organizing groups in his class, should he move to a single presentation?

REFERENCES

Allen, D., and Ryan, K. *Microteaching.* Reading, Mass.: Addison-Wesley, 1969.

Almy, M. *Ways of studying children.* New York: Teachers College Press, Columbia University, 1959.

Amidon, E., and Flanders, N. *The role of the teacher in the classroom.* Minneapolis: Association for Productive Teaching, 1967.

Amidon, E. J., and Hough, J. B. (Eds.). *Interaction analysis: Theory, research, and application.* Reading, Mass.: Addison-Wesley, 1967.

Armstrong, R., Cornell, T., Kraner, R., and Roberson, E. W. *The development and evaluation of behavioral objects.* Worthington, Ohio: Charles A. Jones, 1970.

Bany, M., and Johnson, L. *Classroom group behavior.* New York: Macmillan, 1964.

Blackham, G. *The deviant child in the classroom.* Belmont, Calif.: Wadsworth, 1968.

Bloom, B. S., Engelhart, M. D., Furst, E. J., Hill, W. H., and Krathwohl, D. R. *Taxonomy of educational objectives: The cognitive domain.* Handbook 1. New York: Longmans, 1956.

Borg, W., Kelley, M., Langer, P., and Gall, M. *A microteaching approach to teacher education.* Riverside, N.J.: Macmillan Educational Services, 1970.

Brophy, J., and Good, T. L. Teachers' communication of differential expectations for children's classroom performance: Some behavioral data. *Journal of Educational Psychology,* 1970, *61,* 365–374.

Clarizio, H. F. *Toward positive classroom discipline.* New York: Wiley, 1971.

Dreikurs, R. *Psychology in the classroom.* New York: Harper & Row, 1968.

Eash, M. J. Grouping: What have we learned? In A. Morgenstern (Ed.), *Grouping in the Elementary School.* New York: Pitman, 1966.

Elkind, D. Cognitive development in adolescence. In J. F. Adams (Ed.), *Understanding adolescence.* Boston: Allyn and Bacon, 1968.

Fader, D., and McNeil, E. *Hooked on books: Program and proof.* Berkeley, Calif.: Berkeley Publishing Corporation, 1966.

Fox, R., Luszki, M. B., and Schmuck, R. *Diagnosing classroom learning environments.* Chicago: Science Research Associates, 1966.

Gagné, R. M. *The conditions of learning.* New York: Holt, Rinehart and Winston, 1965.

Gagné, R. M. *The conditions of learning* (2nd ed.). New York: Holt, Rinehart and Winston, 1970.

Gagné, R. M. Some new views of learning and instruction. *Phi Delta Kappan,* 1970, *51,* 468–472.

Gall, M. The use of questions in teaching. *Review of Educational Research,* 1970, *40,* 707–721.

Ginott, H. *Between parent and child.* New York: Avon, 1965.

Ginsburg, H., and Opper, S. *Piaget's theory of intellectual development: An introduction.* Englewood Cliffs, N.J.: Prentice-Hall, 1969.

Glasser, W. *Schools without failure.* New York: Harper & Row, 1969.

Good, T. L. Which pupils do teachers call on? *Elementary School Journal,* 1970, *70,* 190–198.

Greenwood, G. E., Good, T. L., and Siegel, B. L. *Problem situations in teaching.* New York: Harper & Row, 1971.

Holt, J. *How children fail.* New York: Delta, 1964.

Hunter, M. *Motivation theory for teachers.* El Segundo, Calif.: Theory into Practice Publications, 1967.

Hunter, M. *Teacher more—faster!* El Segundo, Calif.: Theory into Practice Publications, 1969.

Hymes, J. *Behavior and misbehavior.* Englewood Cliffs, N.J.: Prentice-Hall, 1955.

Inhelder, B., and Piaget, J. *The growth of logical thinking from childhood to adolescence.* New York: Basic Books, 1958.

Jackson, P. *Life in classrooms.* New York: Holt, Rinehart and Winston, 1968.

Karpus, R. The science curriculum improvement study. In R. E. Ripple and V. N. Rockcastle (Eds.), *Piaget rediscovered.* Ithaca, N.Y.: Cornell University, 1964.

Kephart, N. *The slow learner in the classroom.* Columbus, Ohio: Charles E. Merrill, 1960.

Kounin, J. S., and Gump, P. V. The ripple effect in discipline. *Elementary School Journal,* 1958, *59,* 158–162.

Kounin, J. S., and Gump, P. V. The comparative influence of punitive and non-punitive teachers upon children's concepts of school misconduct. *Journal of Educational Psychology,* 1961, *52,* 44–49.

Lee, D., and Allen, R. *Learning to read through experience* (2nd ed.). New York: Appleton-Century-Crofts, 1963.

Lefever, C. Teachers' characteristics and careers. *Review of Educational Research,* 1967, *37,* 433–444.

Lott, A., and Lott, B. The formation of positive attitude toward group members. *Journal of Abnormal and Social Psychology,* 1960, *61,* 297–300.

Lott, A., and Lott, B. Group cohesiveness, communication level, and conformity. *Journal of Abnormal and Social Psychology,* 1961, *62,* 408–412.

McCandless, B. R. *Children: Behavior and development* (2nd ed.). New York: Holt, Rinehart and Winston, 1967.

McDonald, B., and Nelson L. *Successful classroom control.* Dubuque, Iowa: William C. Brown, 1955.

McDonald, F., and Allen, D. *Training effects on feedback and modeling procedures on teacher performance.* Final Report on U.S.O.E. Project OE-6-10-0178. Stanford University, Stanford, Calif., 1967.

Maslow, J. A. *Motivation and personality* (2nd ed.). New York: Harper & Row, 1970.

Piaget, J. *Play, dreams, and imitation in childhood.* New York: W. W. Norton, 1952.

Rosenthal, R., and Jacobson, L. *Pygmalion in the classroom.* New York: Holt, Rinehart and Winston, 1968.

Russell, D. H., and Russell, E. F. *Listening aids through the grades.* New York: Teachers College Press, Columbia University, 1959.

Sanders, N. *Classroom questions: What kinds?* New York: Harper & Row, 1966.

Schmuck, R., Chesler, M., and Lippitt, R. *Problem solving to improve classroom learning.* Chicago: Science Research Associates, 1966.

Smith, L. M., and Hudgins, B. B. *Educational psychology.* New York: Knopf, 1964.

Smith, L. M., and Geoffrey, W. *The complexities of an urban classroom.* New York: Holt, Rinehart and Winston, 1968.

Stahl, D. K., and Anzalone, P. *Individualized teaching in elementary schools.* West Nyack, N.Y.: Parker Publishing Co., 1970.

Stanchfield, Jo. Personal communication, 1969.

Tiedt, S., and Tiedt, I. *Elementary teacher's complete ideas handbook.* Englewood Cliffs, N.J.: Prentice-Hall, 1965.

White, W. F. *Psychosocial principles applied to classroom teaching.* New York: McGraw-Hill, 1969.

Wiegand, V. K. A study of subordinate skills in science problem solving. Unpublished doctoral dissertation, University of California, Berkeley, 1969.

BIBLIOGRAPHY

The following bibliography should prove useful in classroom problem solving. It is arranged in descending order of importance of the entries.

DIAGNOSING AND ANALYZING PROBLEM SITUATIONS

Brubaker, D. L. *The teacher as a decision-maker.* Dubuque, Iowa: William C. Brown, 1970.

Schmuck, R., Chesler, M., and Lippitt, R. *Problem solving to improve classroom learning.* Chicago: Science Research Associates, 1966.

Fox, R., Luszki, M., and Schmuck, R. *Diagnosing classroom learning environments.* Chicago: Science Research Associates, 1966.

Almy, M. *Ways of studying children.* New York: Teachers College Press, Columbia University, 1959.

Gordon, I. *Studying the child in the school.* New York: Wiley, 1966.

Sawin, E. *Evaluation and the work of the teacher.* Belmont, Calif.: Wadsworth, 1969.

Simpson, R. *Teacher self-evaluation.* New York: Macmillan, 1966.

Rothney, J. *Methods of studying the individual child.* Waltham, Mass.: Blaisdell, 1968.

Bacon, D., and Bernard, H. *Evaluation technique for classroom teachers.* New York: McGraw-Hill, 1958.

Allen, P., Barnes, W., Reese, J., and Roberson, E. *Teacher self-appraisal: A way of looking over your own shoulder.* Worthington, Ohio: Charles A. Jones, 1970.

Amidon, E., and Hunter, E. *Improving teaching.* New York: Holt, Rinehart and Winston, 1966.

GENERAL READING

Kohl, H. *36 children.* New York: Signet, 1967.

Greenberg, H. *Teaching with feeling.* New York: Macmillan, 1969.

Borton, R. *Reach, touch, and teach.* New York: McGraw-Hill, 1970.

James, D. *The taming.* New York: McGraw-Hill, 1969.

Holt, J. *How children learn.* New York: Pitman, 1967.

Holt, J. *How children fail.* New York: Dell, 1964.

Holt, J. *What do I do Monday?* New York: E. P. Dutton, 1970.

Holt, J. *The underachieving school.* New York: Pitman, 1969.

Mager, R. *Developing attitudes toward learning.* Belmont, Calif.: Fearon, 1968.

Hyman, R. *Ways of teaching.* Philadelphia: Lippincott, 1970.

Montessori, M. *The Montessori method.* New York: Schocken Books, 1964.

Postman, N., and Weingartner, C. *Teaching as a subversive activity.* New York: Delacorte, 1969.

TEACHING AND CHILDREN'S THINKING

Raths, L. E., *et al. Teaching for thinking.* Columbus, Ohio: Charles E. Merrill, 1967.

Almy, M. *Young children's thinking.* New York: Teachers College Press, 1966.

Phillips, J., Jr. *Origins of intellect: Piaget's theory.* San Francisco: W. H. Freeman, 1969.

Ginsburg, H., and Opper, S. *Piaget's theory of intellectual development: An introduction.* Englewood Cliffs, N.J.: Prentice-Hall, 1969.

Furth, H. G. *Piaget for teachers.* Englewood Cliffs, N.J.: Prentice-Hall, 1970.

Sullivan, E. *Piaget and the school curriculum: A critical appraisal.* Ontario, Canada: The Ontario Institute for Studies in Education, Bulletin No. 2, 1967.

BEHAVIOR MODIFICATION AND DISCIPLINE

Clarizio, H. F. *Toward positive classroom discipline.* New York: Wiley, 1971.

Gnagey, W. J. *The psychology of discipline in the classroom.* New York: Macmillan, 1968.

Webster, S. W. *Discipline in the classroom.* San Francisco: Chandler, 1968.

Woody, R. H. *Behavioral problems of children in the schools.* New York: Appleton-Century-Crofts, 1969.

Kounin, J. *Discipline and group management in classrooms.* New York: Holt, Rinehart and Winston, 1970.

Meacham, M., and Wiesen, A. *Changing classroom behavior: A manual for precision teaching.* Scranton, Pa.: International Textbook Company, 1970.

Patterson, G., and Guillion, M. *Living with children: New methods for parents and teachers.* Champaign, Ill.: Research Press, 1968.

Brown, D. *Changing student behavior: A new approach to discipline.* Dubuque, Iowa: William C. Brown, 1971.

BEHAVIORAL OBJECTIVES

McAshan, H. H. *Writing behavioral objectives: A new approach.* New York: Harper & Row, 1970.

Kibler, R., Barker, L., and Miles, D. *Behavioral objectives and instruction.* Boston: Allyn and Bacon, 1970.

Mager, R. *Preparing instructional objectives.* Belmont, Calif.: Fearon, 1962.

Gronlund, N. *Stating behavioral objectives for classroom instruction.* New York: Macmillan, 1970.

Armstrong, R., Cornell, T., Kraner, R., and Roberson, E. *The development and evaluation of behavioral objectives.* Worthington, Ohio: Charles A. Jones, 1970.

JOURNALS

Arithmetic Teacher
Art Education
Childhood Education
Children
Education
Educational Leadership
Elementary English
Elementary School Journal
Grade Teacher
Harvard Educational Review
Journal of Educational Psychology
Journal of Reading
Kindergarten
Mathematics Teacher
Education Today
Reading Teacher
Review of Educational Research
School Review
Science Teacher
Social Education
Phi Delta Kappan

INDEX